On Core
Mathematics

Middle School Grade 8

HOUGHTON MIFFLIN HARCOURT

Printed in the U.S.A.

ISBN 978-0-547-57526-1

8 9 10   1409 20 19 18 17 16 15 14 13 12

4500377125   B C D E F G

Table of Contents Grade 8

Unit 1 Expressions and the Number System

Unit 2 Functions

Learning the Common Core State Standards

Has your state adopted the Common Core standards? If so, then you'll be learning both mathematical content standards and the mathematical practice standards that underlie them. The supplementary material found in *On Core Mathematics Grade 8* will help you succeed with both.

> Here are some of the special features you'll find in *On Core Mathematics Grade 8.*

INTERACTIVE LESSONS

You actively participate in every aspect of a lesson. You carry out an activity in an Explore and complete the solution of an Example. This interactivity promotes a deeper understanding of the mathematics.

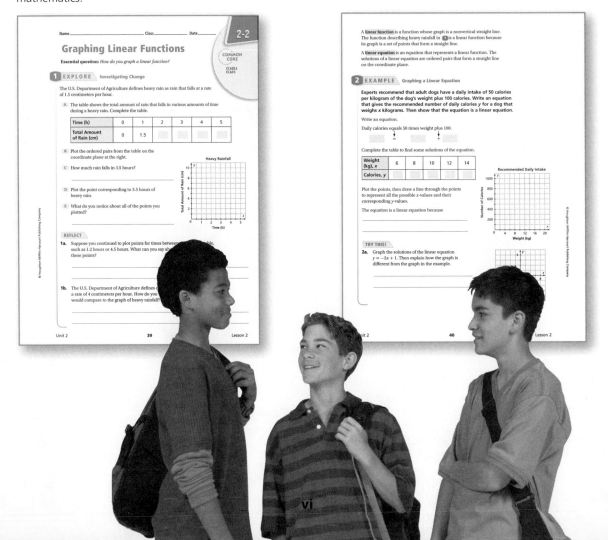

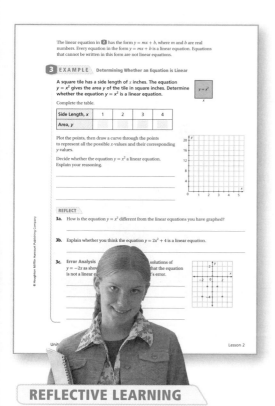

REFLECTIVE LEARNING

You learn to be a reflective thinker through the follow-up questions after each Explore and Example in a lesson. The Reflect questions challenge you to really think about the mathematics you have just encountered and to share your understanding with the class.

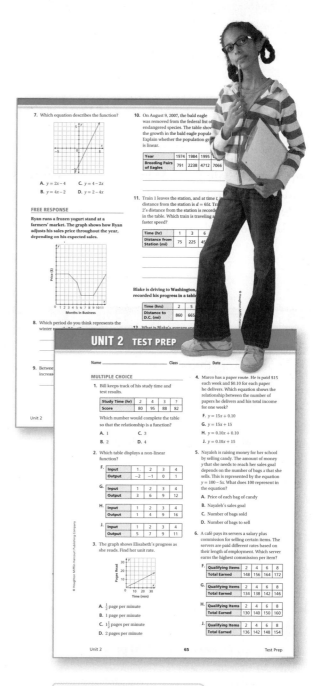

TEST PREP

At the end of a unit, you have an opportunity to practice the material in multiple choice and free response formats common on standardized tests.

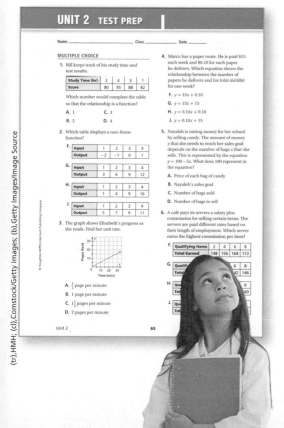

PROBLEM SOLVING CONNECTIONS

Special features that focus on problem solving occur near the ends of units. They help you pull together the mathematical concepts and skills taught in a unit and apply them to real-world situations.

Learning the Standards for Mathematical Practice

The Common Core State Standards include eight Standards for Mathematical Practice. Here's how *On Core Mathematics Grade 8* helps you learn those standards as you master the Standards for Mathematical Content.

1 Make sense of problems and persevere in solving them.

In *On Core Mathematics Grade 8,* you will work through Explores and Examples that present a solution pathway for you to follow. You are asked questions along the way so that you gain an understanding of the solution process, and then you will apply what you've learned in the Try This and Practice for the lesson.

> **3 EXAMPLE**   Writing a Number in Standard Notation
>
> Write each number in standard notation.
>
> A 4.18549×10^{12}
>
>   What is the exponent of the power of 10? _____
>
>   Which direction should you move the decimal point? _____
>
>   Place the decimal point. Add placeholder zeros if necessary.
>
>   _ _ _ _ _ _ _ 4 1 8 5 4 9 _ _ _ _ _ _ _
>
>   The number 4.18549×10^{12} written in standard notation is _____.
>
> B 2.568×10^{-6}
>
>   What is the exponent of the power of 10? _____
>
>   Which direction should you move the decimal point? _____
>
>   Place the decimal point. Add placeholder zeros if necessary.

> Write each number in standard notation.
>
> **9.** 4×10^{5} **10.** 1.8499×10^{9}
>
> **11.** 8.3×10^{-4} **12.** 3.582×10^{-6}

2 Reason abstractly and quantitatively.

When you solve a real-world problem in *On Core Mathematics Grade 8,* learn to represent the situation symbolically by translating the problem into a mathematical expression or equation. You will use these mathematical models to solve the problem and then state your answer in terms of the problem context. You will reflect on the solution process in order to check your answer for reasonableness and to draw conclusions.

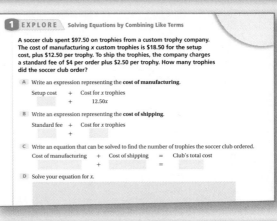

> **1 EXPLORE**   Solving Equations by Combining Like Terms
>
> A soccer club spent $97.50 on trophies from a custom trophy company. The cost of manufacturing x custom trophies is $18.50 for the setup cost, plus $12.50 per trophy. To ship the trophies, the company charges a standard fee of $4 per order plus $2.50 per trophy. How many trophies did the soccer club order?
>
> A   Write an expression representing the **cost of manufacturing**.
>
>   Setup cost   +   Cost for x trophies
>   + $12.50x$
>
> B   Write an expression representing the **cost of shipping**.
>
>   Standard fee   +   Cost for x trophies
>   +
>
> C   Write an equation that can be solved to find the number of trophies the soccer club ordered.
>
>   Cost of manufacturing   +   Cost of shipping   =   Club's total cost
>   +   =
>
> D   Solve your equation for x.

> REFLECT
>
> **1.**   How can you check your answer?

③ Construct viable arguments and critique the reasoning of others.

Throughout *On Core Mathematics Grade 8* you will be asked to make conjectures, construct a mathematical argument, explain your reasoning, and justify your conclusions. Reflect questions offer opportunities for cooperative learning and class discussion. You will have additional opportunities to critique reasoning in Error Analysis problems.

2b. **Conjecture** Do you think that the value of r in the point $(1, r)$ is always the unit rate for any situation? Explain.

7. **Error Analysis** A student claims that the equation $y = 7$ is not a linear equation because it does not have the form $y = mx + b$. Do you agree or disagree? Why?

④ Model with mathematics.

On Core Mathematics Grade 8 presents problems in a variety of contexts such as as science, business, and everyday life. You will use mathematical models such as expressions, equations, tables, and graphs to represent the information in the problem and to solve the problem. Then you will interpret your results in the problem context.

2 EXPLORE Comparing a Table and an Equation

Josh and Maggie buy MP3 files from different music download services. With both services, the monthly charge is a linear function of the number of songs downloaded. The cost at Josh's service is described by $y = 0.50x + 10$ where y is the cost in dollars and x is the number of songs downloaded.

Cost of MP3s at Maggie's Music Service					
Songs, x	5	10	15	20	25
Cost ($), y	4.95	9.90	14.85	19.80	24.75

A Find the unit rate of each function.

Josh: _____ Maggie: _____

B Which function has the greater rate of change? What does that mean in this context?

C Write an equation in slope-intercept form to describe the cost at Maggie's music service.

$y = mx + b$

▢ = ▢ · ▢ + b   *Substitute for y, m, and b.*

▢ = ▢ + b   *Subtract the number that is added*
                         to b from both sides.
− ▢   − ▢

▢ = b

$y =$ ▢ $x +$ ▢

D Describe each service's cost in words using the meanings of the slopes and y-intercepts.

REFLECT

You will use a variety of tools in *On Core Mathematics Grade 8*, including manipulatives, paper and pencil, and technology. You might use manipulatives to develop concepts, paper and pencil to practice skills, and technology (such as graphing calculators, spreadsheets, or geometry software) to investigate more complicated mathematical ideas.

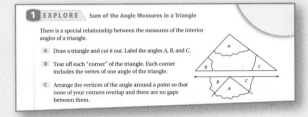

1 EXPLORE   Applying Translations

The triangle is the preimage (input). The arrow shows the motion of a translation and how point A is translated to point A'.

A   Trace the triangle on a piece of paper. Slide point A of your traced triangle down the arrow to model the translation.

B   Sketch the image (output) of the translation.

C   Describe the motion modeled by the translation.

Move _____ units right and _____ units down.

D   Complete the ordered pairs to describe the effect of the translation on point A.

$(1, 11)$ becomes $\left(1 + \boxed{}, 11 + \boxed{}\right) = \left(\boxed{}, \boxed{}\right)$

E   You can give a general rule for a translation by telling the number of units to move up or down and the number of units to move left or right. Complete the ordered pairs to write a general rule for this transformation.

$(x, y) \rightarrow \left(x + \boxed{}, y + \boxed{}\right)$

1 EXPLORE   Sum of the Angle Measures in a Triangle

There is a special relationship between the measures of the interior angles of a triangle.

A   Draw a triangle and cut it out. Label the angles A, B, and C.

B   Tear off each "corner" of the triangle. Each corner includes the vertex of one angle of the triangle.

C   Arrange the vertices of the angle around a point so that none of your corners overlap and there are no gaps between them.

1 EXPLORE   Parallel Lines and Transversals

Use geometry software to explore the angles formed when a transversal intersects parallel lines.

A   Construct a line and label two points on the line A and B.

B   Create point C not on $\overleftrightarrow{AB}$. Then construct a line parallel to $\overleftrightarrow{AB}$ through point C. Create another point on this line and label it D.

Precision refers not only to the correctness of arithmetic calculations, algebraic manipulations, and geometric reasoning but also to the proper use of mathematical language, symbols, and units to communicate mathematical ideas. Throughout *On Core Mathematics Grade 8* you will demonstrate your skills in these areas when you are asked to calculate, describe, show, explain, prove, and predict.

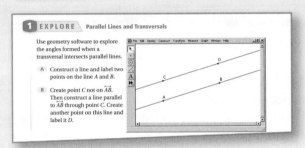

REFLECT

4a. Scientists captured and released a whale shark that weighed about 6×10^5 units. Circle the best choice for the units this measurement is given in: ounces/pounds/tons.

4b. Explain how you chose a unit of measurement in **4a.**

_____

_____

2c. Use your answers to **2a** and **2b** to explain whey there is only one cube root of a positive number.

_____

_____

_____

In *On Core Mathematics Grade 8,* you will look for patterns or regularity in mathematical structures such as expressions, equations, operations, geometric figures, and diagrams. You will use these patterns to generalize beyond a specific case and to make connections between related problems.

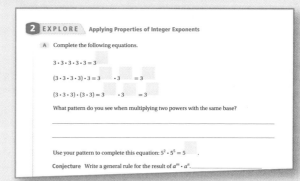

2 **EXPLORE** Applying Properties of Integer Exponents

A Complete the following equations.

$3 \cdot 3 \cdot 3 \cdot 3 \cdot 3 = 3$

$(3 \cdot 3 \cdot 3 \cdot 3) \cdot 3 = 3 \qquad \cdot 3 \qquad = 3$

$(3 \cdot 3 \cdot 3) \cdot (3 \cdot 3) = 3 \qquad \cdot 3 \qquad = 3$

What pattern do you see when multiplying two powers with the same base?

_____

_____

Use your pattern to complete this equation: $5^2 \cdot 5^5 = 5$.

Conjecture Write a general rule for the result of $a^m \cdot a^n$. _____

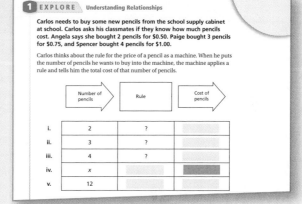

CC.8.F.1

1 **EXPLORE** Understanding Relationships

Carlos needs to buy some new pencils from the school supply cabinet at school. Carlos asks his classmates if they know how much pencils cost. Angela says she bought 2 pencils for $0.50. Paige bought 3 pencils for $0.75, and Spencer bought 4 pencils for $1.00.

Carlos thinks about the rule for the price of a pencil as a machine. When he puts the number of pencils he wants to buy into the machine, the machine applies a rule and tells him the total cost of that number of pencils.

	Number of pencils	Rule	Cost of pencils
i.	2	?	
ii.	3	?	
iii.	4	?	
iv.	x		
v.	12		

Expressions and the Number System

Unit Focus

In this unit, you will learn more about the nature of expressions and the number system. You will learn how to use the properties of integer exponents. You will also learn how to write very small and very large numbers in scientific notation, including performing operations ($+$, $-$, $\times$, $\div$) using scientific notation. You will use your knowledge of exponents to find square roots and cube roots. Lastly, you will learn to determine which numbers are rational and which are irrational. You will then compare the approximation of irrational numbers using decimals and the number line.

Unit at a Glance

COMMON
CORE

UNIT 1

Unpacking the Common Core State Standards

Use the table to help you understand the Standards for Mathematical Content that are taught in this unit. Refer to the lessons listed after each standard for exploration and practice.

COMMON CORE Standards for Mathematical Content	What It Means For You
CC.8.NS.1 Know that numbers that are not rational are called irrational. Understand informally that every number has a decimal expansion; for rational numbers show that the decimal expansion repeats eventually, and convert a decimal expansion which repeats eventually into a rational number. Lesson 1-5	You will learn the definition of an irrational number. You will write rational numbers as decimals.
CC.8.NS.2 Use rational approximations of irrational numbers to compare the size of irrational numbers, locate them approximately on a number line diagram, and estimate the value of expressions (e.g., π^2). Lesson 1-6	You will approximate the value of numbers like $\sqrt{2}$ and locate them on a number line. Then you will order irrational numbers by approximating their values and comparing their locations on a number line.
CC.8.EE.1 Know and apply the properties of integer exponents to generate equivalent numerical expressions. Lesson 1-1	You will look for patterns and make conjectures about properties of exponents. You will explore three properties of exponents and simplify expressions involving powers with positive and negative exponents.
CC.8.EE.2 Use square root and cube root symbols to represent solutions to equations of the form $x^2 = p$ and $x^3 = p$, where p is a positive rational number. Evaluate square roots of small perfect squares and cube roots of small perfect cubes. Know that $\sqrt{2}$ is irrational. Lessons 1-4, 1-6	You will find square roots and cube roots. You will explore why the square root of a number yields two values while the cube root of a number yields only one value.
CC.8.EE.3 Use numbers expressed in the form of a single digit times an integer power of 10 to estimate very large or very small quantities, and to express how many times as much one is than the other. Lesson 1-2	You will learn how to write very small and very large numbers in scientific notation. You will learn that, in scientific notation, positive powers of 10 correspond to numbers greater than 1 and negative exponents correspond to numbers less than 1. You will compare numbers written in scientific notation.
CC.8.EE.4 Perform operations with numbers expressed in scientific notation, including problems where both decimal and scientific notation are used. Use scientific notation and choose units of appropriate size for measurements of very large or very small quantities. … Interpret scientific notation that has been generated by technology. Lesson 1-3	You will perform operations ($+$, $-$, $\times$, $\div$) with numbers written in scientific notation. You will learn how to use a calculator to input and perform operations with numbers written in scientific notation.

Integer Exponents

Essential question: *How can you develop and use the properties of integer exponents?*

COMMON CORE

CC.8.EE.1

1 EXPLORE Using Patterns of Integer Exponents

The table below shows powers of 5, 4, and 3.

$5^4 = 625$	$5^3 = 125$	$5^2 = 25$	$5^1 = 5$	$5^0 =$	$5^{-1} =$	$5^{-2} =$
$4^4 = 256$	$4^3 = 64$	$4^2 = 16$	$4^1 = 4$	$4^0 =$	$4^{-1} =$	$4^{-2} =$
$3^4 = 81$	$3^3 = 27$	$3^2 = 9$	$3^1 = 3$	$3^0 =$	$3^{-1} =$	$3^{-2} =$

A What pattern do you see in the powers of 5?

_____

_____

B What pattern do you see in the powers of 4?

_____

_____

C Complete the table for the values of $5^0, 5^{-1}, 5^{-2}$.

D Complete the table for the values of $4^0, 4^{-1}, 4^{-2}$.

E Complete the table for the values of $3^0, 3^{-1}, 3^{-2}$.

F **Conjecture** Write a general rule for the values of a^0 and a^{-n} based on the patterns in the table.

_____

TRY THIS!

Find the value of each power.

1a. 6^{-4} **1b.** 12^0 **1c.** 8^{-1} **1d.** 7^{-3}

_____ _____ _____ _____

1e. 347^0 **1f.** 15^{-2} **1g.** 20^2 **1h.** 6^{-5}

_____ _____ _____ _____

2 EXPLORE Applying Properties of Integer Exponents

A Complete the following equations.

$$3 \cdot 3 \cdot 3 \cdot 3 \cdot 3 = 3^{\boxed{}}$$

$$(3 \cdot 3 \cdot 3 \cdot 3) \cdot 3 = 3^{\boxed{}} \cdot 3^{\boxed{}} = 3^{\boxed{}}$$

$$(3 \cdot 3 \cdot 3) \cdot (3 \cdot 3) = 3^{\boxed{}} \cdot 3^{\boxed{}} = 3^{\boxed{}}$$

What pattern do you see when multiplying two powers with the same base?

_____

_____

Use your pattern to complete this equation: $5^2 \cdot 5^5 = 5^{\boxed{}}$.

Conjecture Write a general rule for the result of $a^m \cdot a^n$. _____

B Complete the following equation: $\dfrac{4^5}{4^3} = \dfrac{4 \cdot 4 \cdot 4 \cdot 4 \cdot 4}{4 \cdot 4 \cdot 4} = \dfrac{\cancel{4} \cdot \cancel{4} \cdot \cancel{4} \cdot 4 \cdot 4}{\cancel{4}_1 \cdot \cancel{4}_1 \cdot \cancel{4}_1} = 4 \cdot 4 = 4^{\boxed{}}$

What pattern do you see when dividing two powers with the same base?

_____

_____

Use your pattern to complete this equation: $\dfrac{6^8}{6^3} = 6^{\boxed{}}$.

Conjecture Write a general rule for the result of $\dfrac{a^m}{a^n}$. _____

C Complete the following equations:

$$\left(5^3\right)^2 = (5 \cdot 5 \cdot 5)^{\boxed{}}$$

$$= (5 \cdot 5 \cdot 5) \cdot (5 \cdot 5 \cdot 5)$$

$$= 5^{\boxed{}}$$

What pattern do you see when raising a power to a power?

_____

_____

Use your pattern to complete this equation: $\left(7^2\right)^4 = 7^{\boxed{}}$.

Conjecture Write a general rule for the result of $\left(a^m\right)^n$. _____

Use properties of exponents to write an equivalent expression.

2a. $9^2 \cdot 9^4$ **2b.** $\dfrac{12^{22}}{12^4}$ **2c.** $\left(4^{10}\right)^5$ **2d.** $\dfrac{6^9}{6^{12}}$

_____   _____   _____   _____

2e. $13^3 \cdot 13^1$ **2f.** $\left(12^4\right)^6$ **2g.** $\dfrac{8^9}{8^4}$ **2h.** $\dfrac{16^5}{16^{12}}$

_____   _____   _____   _____

3 EXAMPLE Applying Properties of Integer Exponents

Simplify each expression.

A $(5-2)^5 \cdot 3^{-8} + (5+2)^0$

$(5-2)^5 \cdot 3^{-8} + (5+2)^0$ *Follow the order of operations.*

$\left(\boxed{}\right)^5 \cdot 3^{-8} + \left(\boxed{}\right)^0$ *Simplify within parentheses.*

$3^{\boxed{}} + \boxed{}$ *Use properties of exponents.*

$3^{\boxed{}} + \boxed{}$ *Simplify.*

$\dfrac{1}{\boxed{}} + \boxed{}$ *Add.*

$1\dfrac{1}{\boxed{}}$

B $(10-6)^3 \cdot 4^2 + (10+2)^2$

$(10-6)^3 \cdot 4^2 + (10+2)^2$ *Follow the order of operations.*

$\left(\boxed{}\right)^3 \cdot 4^2 + \left(\boxed{}\right)^2$ *Simplify within parentheses.*

$4^{\boxed{}} + \boxed{}$ *Use properties of exponents.*

$4^{\boxed{}} + \boxed{}$ *Simplify.*

$\boxed{} + \boxed{}$ *Add.*

$\boxed{}$

Simplify each expression.

3a. $\dfrac{\left[(6-1)^2\right]^2}{(3+2)^3}$ _____   **3b.** $\left(2^2\right)^3 - (10-6)^3 \cdot 4^{-5}$ _____

PRACTICE

Find the value of each power.

1. 7^{-2}

_____

2. 20^0

_____

3. 10^{-3}

_____

4. 2^{-5}

_____

5. 5^{-3}

_____

6. 7^3

_____

Use properties of integers to write an equivalent expression.

7. $15^2 \cdot 15^{-5}$

_____

8. $\dfrac{20^{10}}{20^7}$

_____

9. $\dfrac{14^4}{14^9}$

_____

10. $\left(8^4\right)^{12}$

_____

11. $\left(12^{-5}\right)^3$

_____

12. $4^{-3} \cdot 4^{-21}$

_____

13. $m \cdot m^4$

_____

14. $\dfrac{r^5}{r^2}$

_____

15. $\left(a^3\right)^{-3}$

_____

Find the missing exponent.

16. $b^{\boxed{}} \cdot b^2 = b^8$

17. $\dfrac{x^5}{x^{\boxed{}}} = x^{-2}$

18. $\left(n^{\boxed{}}\right)^4 = n^0$

Simplify each expression.

19. $(2+4)^2 + 8^{-6} \times (12-4)^{10}$ _____

20. $\left(3^3\right)^2 \times \left(\dfrac{(5-2)^3}{3^4}\right) + (10-4)^2 \times 6^{10}$ _____

21. **Error Analysis** A student simplified the expression $\dfrac{4^3}{16^3}$ as $\dfrac{1}{4}$. Do you agree with the student? Justify your answer.

_____

22. Find the values of $x^5 \cdot x^{-3}$ and $\dfrac{x^5}{x^3}$. What do you notice about the two values? Explain why your results make sense based on the properties you learned in this lesson.

_____

Scientific Notation

Essential question: *How can you use scientific notation to express very large and very small quantities?*

COMMON CORE

CC.8.EE.3

Scientific notation is a method of expressing very large and very small numbers as a product of a number greater than or equal to 1 and less than 10, and a power of 10.

1 EXPLORE   Using Scientific Notation

The weights of various sea creatures are shown in the table. You can write the weights in scientific notation.

Sea Creature	Blue Whale	Whale Shark	Eel	Minnow
Weight (lbs)	250,000	41,200	133.25	0.95

Write the weight of the blue whale in scientific notation.

A   Move the decimal point in 250,000 to the left as many places as necessary to find a number that is greater than or equal to 1 and less than 10.

What number did you find? _____

B   Divide 250,000 by your answer to **A** . Write your answer as a power of 10.

_____

C   Combine your answers to **A** and **B** to represent 250,000.

$$250,000 = \boxed{} \times 10^{\boxed{}}$$

Write the weight of the minnow in scientific notation.

D   Move the decimal point in 0.95 to the right as many places as necessary to find a number that is greater than or equal to 1 and less than 10.

What number did you find? _____

E   Divide 0.95 by your answer to **D** . Write your answer as a power of 10.

_____

F   Combine your answers to **D** and **E** to represent 0.95.

$$0.95 = \boxed{} \times 10^{\boxed{}}$$

1a. What do you notice about the sign of the exponent for weights greater than one pound?

_____

1b. What do you notice about the sign of the exponent for weights less than one pound?

_____

To translate between standard notation and scientific notation, you can count the number of places the decimal point moves.

Writing Numbers in Scientific Notation

When the number is greater than or equal to 1, use a positive exponent.	$84,000 = 8.4 \times 10^4$	*The decimal point moves 4 places.*
When the number is less than 1, use a negative exponent.	$0.0783 = 7.83 \times 10^{-2}$	*The decimal point moves 2 places.*

2 EXAMPLE Writing a Number in Scientific Notation

An estimate of the world population in 2010 was 6,880,000,000. Write the world's population in scientific notation.

To write 6,880,000,000 in scientific notation, move the decimal point as many places as necessary to find a number that is greater than or equal to 1 and less than 10.

Place the decimal point: 6 8 8 0 0 0 0 0 0 0

Which direction did you move the decimal point? _____

What number did you find? _____

How many places did you move the decimal point? _____

When 6,880,000,000 is written in scientific notation, should the exponent of the power of 10 be positive or negative? Explain.

_____

_____

The world's population, 6,880,000,000, written in scientific notation is

☐ $\times 10$ ☐   .

To translate between scientific notation and standard notation, you can move the decimal point the number of places indicated by the exponent in the pwoer of 10. When the exponent is positive, move the decimal point to the right. When the exponent is negative, move the decimal point to the left.

3 EXAMPLE Writing a Number in Standard Notation

Write each number in standard notation.

A 4.18549×10^{12}

What is the exponent of the power of 10? _____

Which direction should you move the decimal point? _____

Place the decimal point. Add placeholder zeros if necessary.

— — — — — — 4 1 8 5 4 9 — — — — — — — — —

The number 4.18549×10^{12} written in standard notation is _____.

B 2.568×10^{-6}

What is the exponent of the power of 10? _____

Which direction should you move the decimal point? _____

Place the decimal point. Add placeholder zeros if necessary.

— — — — — — — — — 2 5 6 8 — — — — — —

The number 2.568×10^{-6} written in standard notation is _____.

4 EXAMPLE Comparing Numbers in Scientific Notation

The approximate weight of a whale shark is 4×10^4 pounds. The approximate weight of a common dolphin is 2×10^2 pounds. How many times as great as the weight of the whale shark is the weight of the dolphin?

First compare the values between 1 and 10.

The 4 in 4×10^4 is _____ times as great as the 2 in 2×10^2.

Next compare the powers of 10.

10^4 is _____ times as great as 10^2.

Circle the most reasonable answer.

The weight of the whale shark is 2 / 20 / 200 / 2000 times as great as the weight of the dolphin.

REFLECT

4a. Scientists captured and released a whale shark that weighed about 6×10^5 units. Circle the best choice for the units this measurement is given in: ounces / pounds / tons.

4b. Explain how you chose a unit of measurement in **4a.**

_____

_____

_____

PRACTICE

Write each number in scientific notation.

1. 58,927

_____

2. 1,304,000,000

_____

3. 0.000487

_____

4. 0.000028

_____

5. 0.000059

_____

6. 6,730,000

_____

7. 13,300

_____

8. 0.0417

_____

Write each number in standard notation.

9. 4×10^5

_____

10. 1.8499×10^9

_____

11. 8.3×10^{-4}

_____

12. 3.582×10^{-6}

_____

13. 2.97×10^{-2}

_____

14. 6.41×10^3

_____

15. 8.456×10^7

_____

16. 9.06×10^{-5}

_____

Circle the correct answer.

17. 8×10^5 is 2/20/200/2,000 times as great as 4×10^2.

18. 9×10^{10} is 30/300/3,000/30,000 times as great as 3×10^7.

19. 4×10^{-5} is 0.02/0.2/2/20 times as great as 2×10^{-4}.

20. 4×10^{-12} is 0.00001/0.0001/10/1000 times as great as 4×10^{-8}.

21. The mass of a proton is about 1.7×10^{-24} g. The mass of a neutron is about the same as a proton. The nucleus of an atom of carbon has 6 protons and 6 neutrons. The mass of the nucleus is about 2×10^{-26} units. Circle the best choice for the units this measurement is given in: g/kg/tons

22. The air distance between Los Angeles, California, and New York City, New York, is about 3.9×10^3 units. Circle the best choice for the units this measurement is given in: cm/m/km

Operations with Scientific Notation

COMMON CORE

CC.8.EE.4

Essential question: *How do you add, subtract, multiply, and divide using scientific notation?*

1 EXPLORE Adding and Subtracting with Scientific Notation

The table below shows the population of the three largest countries in North America. Find the total population of the three countries.

Country	United States	Canada	Mexico
Population	3.1×10^8	3.38×10^7	1.1×10^8

Method 1:

A First write each population with the same power of 10.

United States: [   ] × 10[ ]

Canada: [   ] × 10[ ]

Mexico: [   ] × 10[ ]

B Add the multipliers for each population. $3.1 +$ [   ] $+ 1.1 =$ [   ]

C Write the final answer in scientific notation. _____

Method 2:

D First write each number in standard notation.

United States: _____

Canada: _____

Mexico: _____

E Find the sum of the numbers in standard notation.

$310{,}000{,}000 +$ [   ] $+$ [   ] $=$ [   ]

F Write the answer in scientific notation. _____

TRY THIS!

1a. Using the population table above, how many more people live in Mexico than in Canada?

2 EXPLORE Multiplying and Dividing with Scientific Notation

When the sun makes an orbit around the center of the Milky Way, it travels 2.025×10^{14} kilometers. The orbit takes 225 million years. At what rate does the Sun travel around the Milky Way? Write your answer in scientific notation.

A Set up a division problem to represent the situation.

$$\text{Rate} = \frac{\text{Distance}}{\text{Time}}$$

$$\text{Rate} = \frac{\boxed{} \text{ kilometers}}{\boxed{} \text{ years}}$$

B Write 225 million years in scientific notation. _____

C Write the expression for rate with years in scientific notation.

$$\text{Rate} = \frac{\boxed{} \text{ kilometers}}{\boxed{} \text{ years}}$$

D Find the quotient by dividing the multipliers.

$$2.025 \div \boxed{} = \boxed{}$$

E Use the laws of exponents to divide the powers of 10.

$$\frac{10^{14}}{10^{8}} = 10^{\boxed{}} = 10^{\boxed{}}$$

F Combine the answers from **D** and **E** to write the rate in scientific notation.

_____

TRY THIS!

2a. Light from the Sun travels at a speed of 1.86×10^5 miles per second. It takes sunlight about 4.8×10^3 seconds to reach Saturn. Find the approximate distance from the Sun to Saturn. Write your answer in scientific notation.

$$d = rt$$

$$= \left(\boxed{} \times 10^5 \right) \left(\boxed{} \times 10^3 \right)$$

$$= \left(\boxed{} \right) (4.8) \times \left(\boxed{} \right) (10^3)$$

$$= \boxed{} \times 10^{\boxed{}}$$

$$= \boxed{} \times 10^{\boxed{}} \text{ miles}$$

On many scientific calculators, you can enter numbers in scientific notation by using a function labeled "ee" or "EE". Usually, the letter "E" takes the place of "×10". So, the number 4.1×10^9 would appear as 4.1E9 on the calculator.

3 **EXAMPLE** **Scientific Notation on a Calculator**

The table below shows the approximate populations for the three continents with the greatest populations. What is the total population of these three continents? Use your calculator to find the answer.

Continent	Asia	Africa	Europe
Population	4.1×10^9	1.0×10^9	7.28×10^8

Find $4.1 \times 10^9 + 1.0 \times 10^9 + 7.28 \times 10^8$.

Enter 4.1E9 + 1E ____ + ____ E ____ on your calculator.

Write the results from your calculator. _____

Write this number in scientific notation. _____

The total population of the three continents is _____ people.

TRY THIS!

Write each number using calculator notation.

1a. 7.5×10^5

1b. 3×10^{-7}

1c. 2.7×10^{13}

_____   _____   _____

Write each number using scientific notation.

1d. 4.5E−1

1e. 5.6E12

1f. 6.98E−8

_____   _____   _____

PRACTICE

Add or subtract. Write your answer in scientific notation.

1. $3.2 \times 10^5 + 4.9 \times 10^8$

2. $4.378 \times 10^{12} + 7.701 \times 10^7$

_____   _____

3. $2.3 \times 10^8 - 2.12 \times 10^3$

4. $4.55 \times 10^{15} - 7.4 \times 10^{11}$

_____   _____

5. $6.35 \times 10^3 + 1.65 \times 10^6$

6. $5 \times 10^3 - 1.23 \times 10^2$

_____   _____

Multiply or divide. Write your answer in scientific notation.

7. $(1.8 \times 10^9)(6.78 \times 10^{12})$

8. $(5.092 \times 10^{21})(3.38 \times 10^6)$

9. $\dfrac{8.4 \times 10^{21}}{4.2 \times 10^{14}}$

10. $\dfrac{3.46 \times 10^{17}}{2 \times 10^9}$

11. A newborn baby has about 26,000,000,000 cells. An adult has about 1.9×10^3 times as many cells as a newborn. About how many cells does an adult have? Write your answer in scientific notation.

12. The edge of a cube measures 3.5×10^{-2} meters. What is the volume of the cube in cubic meters? Write your answer in scientific notation.

13. The smallest state in the United States is Rhode Island with a land area of about 2.9×10^{10} square feet. The largest state is Alaska whose land area is about 5.5×10^2 as great as the land area of Rhode Island. What is the land area of Alaska in square feet? Write your answer in scientific notation.

14. Astronomers estimate that the diameter of the Andromeda galaxy is approximately 2.2×10^5 light-years. A light-year is the distance light travels in a vacuum in 1 year. One light-year is approximately 5.9×10^{12} miles. What is the diameter of the Andromeda galaxy in miles? Write your answer in scientific notation.

The table below shows the approximate populations of three countries.

Country	China	France	Australia
Population	1.33×10^9	6.48×10^7	2.15×10^7

15. How many more people live in France than in Australia? Write your answer in scientific notation.

16. The area of Australia is about 2.95×10^6 square miles. What is the approximate average number of people per square mile in Australia?

17. What is the ratio of the population of China to the population of France? What does this mean?

Square Roots and Cube Roots

COMMON CORE

CC.8.EE.2

Essential question: *How do you evaluate square roots and cube roots?*

1 **EXPLORE** **Finding the Square Root of Perfect Squares**

There are 9 square tiles used to make a
square mosaic. There are 3 tiles along
each side of the mosaic.

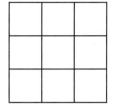

Another square mosaic is made using 64 square tiles. How many tiles are on each
side of this mosaic?

A Use what you know about the mosaic made with 9 tiles to find the relationship
between number of tiles on each side and the total number of square tiles.

_____

_____

B Use this relationship to find the number of tiles along the side of a square
mosaic made of 64 square tiles.

_____

C In this context, the total number of tiles is the number of tiles along each
side of the mosaic squared. When the total number of tiles is 9, the number
of tiles along a side is 3. Because $3^2 = 9$, we call 3 a *square root* of 9. This is
written as $3 = \sqrt{9}$.

Use this notation to write the square root of 64: $\sqrt{64} = $ ▭

TRY THIS!

Evaluate each square root.

1a. $\sqrt{169}$ **1b.** $\sqrt{\dfrac{1}{16}}$ **1c.** $\sqrt{81}$ **1d.** $\sqrt{\dfrac{1}{400}}$

_____   _____   _____   _____

The **square root** of a positive number p is x if $x^2 = p$. There are two square
roots for every positive number. For example, the square roots of 36 are 6 and
-6 because $6^2 = 36$ and $(-6)^2 = 36$. The square roots of $\frac{1}{25}$ are $\frac{1}{5}$ and $-\frac{1}{5}$. You can
write the square roots of $\frac{1}{25}$ as $\pm\frac{1}{5}$. The symbol $\sqrt{}$ indicates the positive,
or **principal square root**.

A number that is a **perfect square** has square roots that are integers. The number
81 is a perfect square because its square roots are 9 and -9.

A cube shaped toy is made of 27 small cubes.
There are 3 cubes along each edge of the toy.

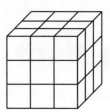

Another cube shaped toy is made using 8 small cubes.
How many small cubes are on each edge of this toy?

A Use what you know about the toy made with 27 small cubes to find the relationship between number of cubes on each edge and the total number of cubes.

_____

_____

_____

B Use this relationship to find the number of small cubes along each edge of a toy made of 8 small cubes.

_____

C In this situation, the total number of small cubes is the number of small cubes along each edge of the toy cubed. When the total number of small cubes is 27, the number of small cubes along each edge is 3. Because $3^3 = 27$, we call 3 a *cube root* of 27. This is written as $\sqrt[3]{27} = 3$.

Use this notation to write the cube root of 8: $\sqrt[3]{8} =$

REFLECT

2a. The product of 3 equal positive factors is positive / negative.

2b. The product of 3 equal negative factors is positive / negative.

2c. Use your answers to **2a** and **2b** to explain whey there is only one cube root of a positive number.

_____

_____

_____

TRY THIS!

Evaluate each cube root.

2d. $\sqrt[3]{125}$ **2e.** $\sqrt[3]{\frac{1}{8}}$ **2f.** $\sqrt[3]{1000}$ **2g.** $\sqrt[3]{\frac{1}{343}}$

_____ _____ _____ _____

The **cube root** of a positive number p is x if $x^3 = p$. There is one cube root for every positive number. For example, the cube root of 8 is 2 because $2^3 = 8$. The cube root of $\frac{1}{27}$ is $\frac{1}{3}$ because $\left(\frac{1}{3}\right)^3 = \frac{1}{27}$. The symbol $\sqrt[3]{}$ indicates the cube root. A number that is a **perfect cube** has a cube root that is an integer. The number 125 is a perfect cube because its cube root is 5.

3 EXAMPLE   Solving Equations Using Square Roots and Cube Roots

Solve each equation for x.

A $x^2 = 121$

$\sqrt{x^2} = \sqrt{121}$ *Solve for x by taking the square root of both sides.*

$x = \sqrt{121}$ *Think: What number squared equals 121?*

$x = \pm \boxed{}$ *Use $\pm$ to show both square roots.*

The solutions are _____ and _____.

B $x^2 = \frac{16}{169}$

$\sqrt{x^2} = \sqrt{\frac{16}{169}}$ *Solve for x by taking the square root of both sides.*

$x = \sqrt{\frac{16}{169}}$ *Think: What number squared equals $\frac{16}{169}$?*

$x = \pm \dfrac{4}{\boxed{}}$ *Use $\pm$ to show both square roots.*

The solutions are _____ and _____.

C $729 = x^3$

$\sqrt[3]{729} = \sqrt[3]{x^3}$ *Solve for x by taking the cube root of both sides.*

$\sqrt[3]{729} = x$ *Think: What number cubed equals 729?*

$\boxed{} = x$

The solution is _____.

D $x^3 = \frac{8}{125}$

$\sqrt[3]{x^3} = \sqrt[3]{\frac{8}{125}}$ *Solve for x by taking the cube root of both sides.*

$x = \sqrt[3]{\frac{8}{125}}$ *Think: What number cubed equals $\frac{8}{125}$?*

$x = \dfrac{2}{\boxed{}}$

The solution is _____.

PRACTICE

Find the square roots of each number.

1. 144 _____

2. 256 _____

3. $\frac{1}{81}$ _____

4. $\frac{49}{900}$ _____

5. 400 _____

6. $\frac{1}{100}$ _____

Find the cube root of each number.

7. 216 _____

8. 8000 _____

9. $\frac{27}{125}$ _____

10. $\frac{1}{27}$ _____

11. $\frac{27}{64}$ _____

12. 512 _____

Simplify each expression.

13. $\sqrt{16} + \sqrt{25}$ _____

14. $\sqrt[3]{125} + 10$ _____

15. $\sqrt{25} + 10$ _____

16. $8 - \sqrt{64}$ _____

17. $\sqrt[3]{\frac{16}{2}} + 1$ _____

18. $\sqrt{\frac{16}{4}} + \sqrt{4}$ _____

19. The foyer of Ann's house is a square with an area of 36 square feet. What is the length of each side of the foyer?

_____

20. A chessboard has 32 black squares and 32 white squares arranged in a square. How many squares are along each side of the chessboard?

_____

21. A cubic aquarium holds 27 cubic feet of water. What is the length of each edge of the cube?

_____

22. **Reasoning** How can you check your answer when you find the square root(s) of a number?

_____

_____

23. **Reasoning** Can you arrange 12 small squares to make a larger square? Can you arrange 20 small cubes to make a larger cube? Explain how this relates to perfect squares and perfect cubes.

_____

_____

Rational Numbers

COMMON CORE

CC.8.NS.1

Essential question: *How do you write rational numbers as decimals and as fractions?*

A **rational number** is a number that can be written as a ratio in the form $\frac{a}{b}$, where a and b are integers and b is not 0.

 EXAMPLE **Writing Fractions as Decimals**

Write each fraction as a decimal.

A $\frac{1}{4}$

$$\begin{array}{r} 0.2 \\ 4\overline{)1.0\,0} \\ -8 \\ \hline 2 \\ - \\ \hline \end{array}$$

Remember that the fraction bar means "divided by." Divide the numerator by the denominator.

Divide until the remainder is 0, adding zeros after the decimal point in the dividend as needed.

$\frac{1}{4} =$ _____

B $\frac{1}{3}$

$$\begin{array}{r} 0.3 \\ \overline{)1.0\,0\,0} \\ - \\ \hline \\ - \\ \hline \\ - \\ \hline \end{array}$$

Will this division ever end in a remainder of 0? Explain.

_____

Describe the quotient.

_____

When a decimal has one or more digits that repeat indefinitely, write the decimal with a bar over the repeating digit(s).

$\frac{1}{3} =$ _____

Write each fraction as a decimal.

1a. $\frac{5}{11}$

1b. $\frac{1}{8}$

1c. $\frac{4}{5}$

_____

_____

_____

REFLECT

1c. How do you write $1\frac{1}{4}$ as a decimal?

_____

1d. How do you write $2\frac{1}{3}$ as a decimal?

_____

The examples in **1** show the two kinds of decimals that represent rational numbers.

- After the decimal point, there may be a finite number of digits. This is called a terminating decimal. 0.25 is a **terminating decimal**.

- After the decimal point, there may be a block of one or more digits that are not all zero that repeat indefinitely. This is called a repeating decimal. $0.\overline{3}$ is a **repeating decimal**.

Every rational number can be written as a terminating decimal or a repeating decimal.

2 EXAMPLE   **Writing Decimals as Fractions**

Write each decimal as a fraction in simplest form.

A   0.825

The decimal 0.825 means "825 thousandths." Write this as a fraction.

$$\frac{\boxed{}}{\boxed{}}$$

Then simplify the fraction.

$$\frac{825 \div \boxed{}}{1000 \div \boxed{}} = \frac{\boxed{}}{40}$$

$$0.825 = \frac{\boxed{}}{\boxed{}}$$

B $0.\overline{37}$

Let $x = 0.\overline{37}$. $0.\overline{37}$ has _____ repeating digits, so multiply each side of the equation $x = 0.\overline{37}$ by 10^2, or _____.

Because $x = 0.\overline{37}$, you can subtract x from one side and $0.\overline{37}$ from the other. ⟶

To solve for x, divide both sides of the equation by _____. Then simplify if necessary. ⟶

$$x = 0.\overline{37}$$
$$(100)x = (100)\, 0.\overline{37}$$
$$100x = 37.\overline{37}$$
$$\frac{-x \quad -0.\overline{37}}{99x = 37}$$
$$\frac{99x}{} = \frac{37}{}$$
$$x = \frac{}{}$$

$$0.\overline{37} = \frac{}{}$$

REFLECT

2a. How do you know that 0.825 and $0.\overline{37}$ can be written as fractions?

_____

_____

TRY THIS!

Write each decimal as a fraction in simplest form.

2b. 0.12 _____ **2c.** $0.\overline{57}$ _____ **2d.** 1.4 _____

PRACTICE

Write each fraction as a decimal.

1. $\dfrac{7}{8}$

_____

2. $\dfrac{2}{3}$

_____

3. $2\dfrac{4}{5}$

_____

4. $\dfrac{23}{24}$

_____

5. $\dfrac{17}{20}$

_____

6. $\dfrac{18}{25}$

_____

Write each decimal as a fraction in simplest form.

7. $7.\overline{4}$ _____

8. 0.56 _____

9. 0.45 _____

10. $0.\overline{93}$ _____

11. $0.\overline{54}$ _____

12. 6.02 _____

Compare. Write <, >, or =.

13. $\frac{4}{7}$ ◯ $\frac{3}{8}$

14. $\frac{3}{4}$ ◯ 0.75

15. 0.35 ◯ $\frac{1}{3}$

16. $0.\overline{5}$ ◯ $\frac{5}{9}$

17. 1.5 ◯ $1\frac{3}{5}$

18. $\frac{2}{3}$ ◯ 0.67

19. A $\frac{5}{16}$-inch-long bolt is used in a machine. What is the length of the bolt written as a decimal?

_____

20. The average width of a robin's egg is about 0.015 meter. Write this length as a fraction in simplest form.

_____

21. The weight of an object on the moon is $\frac{1}{6}$ its weight on Earth. Write $\frac{1}{6}$ as a decimal.

_____

22. Oxygen makes up about $\frac{3}{5}$ of the human body. Write $\frac{3}{5}$ as a decimal.

_____

23. On a test, Jerry answered 52 out of 60 questions correctly. What portion of Jerry's answers was correct? Write your answer as a decimal.

_____

24. Write $\frac{1}{9}$ and $\frac{2}{9}$ as decimals. Use the results to predict the decimal equivalent of $\frac{8}{9}$.

_____

25. The decimal equivalent of $\frac{1}{25}$ is 0.04, and the decimal equivalent of $\frac{2}{25}$ is 0.08. Without dividing, find the decimal equivalent of $\frac{6}{25}$. Explain how you found your answer.

_____

26. **Conjecture** A number that is not rational is called an irrational number. When written as a decimal, an irrational number is not _____

_____

Name _____ Class _____ Date _____

Irrational Numbers

Essential question: *How do you estimate and compare irrational numbers?*

Irrational numbers are numbers that are not rational. In other words, they cannot be written in the form $\frac{a}{b}$, where a and b are integers and $b \neq 0$. Square roots of integers that are not perfect squares are irrational. Other special numbers, like π, are also irrational.

1 **EXPLORE** Estimating Irrational Numbers

Estimate the value of $\sqrt{2}$.

A Since 2 is not a perfect square, $\sqrt{2}$ is irrational.

To estimate $\sqrt{2}$, first find two consecutive perfect squares that 2 is between. Complete the inequality by writing these perfect squares in the boxes.

Now take the square root of each number.

Simplify the square roots of perfect squares.

$\boxed{} < 2 < \boxed{}$

$\sqrt{\boxed{}} < \sqrt{2} < \sqrt{\boxed{}}$

$\boxed{} < \sqrt{2} < \boxed{}$

$\sqrt{2}$ is between _____ and _____.

Estimate that $\sqrt{2} \approx 1.5$.

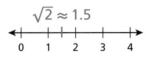

$\sqrt{2} \approx 1.5$

0 1 2 3 4

B To find a better estimate, first choose some numbers between 1 and 2 and square them. For example, choose 1.3, 1.4, and 1.5.

$1.3^2 =$ _____ $1.4^2 =$ _____ $1.5^2 =$ _____

Is $\sqrt{2}$ between 1.3 and 1.4? How do you know?

_____

Is $\sqrt{2}$ between 1.4 and 1.5? How do you know?

_____

$\sqrt{2}$ is between _____ and _____, so $\sqrt{2} \approx$ _____.

Locate and label this value on the number line.

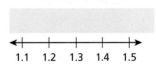

1.1 1.2 1.3 1.4 1.5

REFLECT

1a. How could you find an even better estimate of $\sqrt{2}$?

_____

1b. Use your method from **1a** to find a better estimate of $\sqrt{2}$. Draw a number line and locate and label your estimate.

$\sqrt{2}$ is between _____ and _____, so $\sqrt{2} \approx$ _____.

1c. Estimate the value of $\sqrt{7}$ to the nearest hundredth.
Draw a number line and locate and label your estimate.

$\sqrt{7}$ is between _____ and _____, so $\sqrt{7} \approx$ _____.

2 EXAMPLE   Comparing Irrational Numbers

Compare. Write <, >, or =.

A $\sqrt{3} + 5 \bigcirc 3 + \sqrt{5}$

First approximate $\sqrt{3}$ to the nearest tenth.

$\sqrt{3}$ is between _____ and _____, so $\sqrt{3} \approx$ _____.

Next approximate $\sqrt{5}$ to the nearest tenth.

$\sqrt{5}$ is between _____ and _____, so $\sqrt{5} \approx$ _____.

Then use your approximations to simplify the expressions.

$\sqrt{3} + 5 \bigcirc 3 + \sqrt{5}$

$\boxed{} + 5 \bigcirc 3 + \boxed{}$ *Substitute your approximations.*

$\boxed{} \bigcirc \boxed{}$ *Simplify, then compare.*

So, $\sqrt{3} + 5 \bigcirc 3 + \sqrt{5}$

B $\sqrt{10} + 2 \bigcirc 10 + \sqrt{2}$

First approximate $\sqrt{10}$ to the nearest tenth.

$\sqrt{10}$ is between _____ and _____, so $\sqrt{10} \approx$ _____.

Next approximate $\sqrt{2}$ to the nearest tenth.

$\sqrt{2}$ is between _____ and _____, so $\sqrt{2} \approx$ _____.

Then use your approximations to simplify the expressions.

$\sqrt{10} + 2 \bigcirc 10 + \sqrt{2}$

$\boxed{} + 2 \bigcirc 10 + \boxed{}$ *Substitute your approximations.*

$\boxed{} \bigcirc \boxed{}$ *Simplify, then compare.*

So, $\sqrt{10} + 2 \bigcirc 10 + \sqrt{2}$

Compare. Write <, >, or =.

2a. $\sqrt{2}+4$ ⬤ $2+\sqrt{4}$

2b. $\sqrt{12}+6$ ⬤ $12+\sqrt{6}$

---

3 **EXAMPLE** **Ordering Irrational Numbers**

Order $\sqrt{3}$, π, and 1.5 from least to greatest.

First approximate $\sqrt{3}$ to the nearest tenth.

$\sqrt{3}$ is between _____ and _____, so $\sqrt{3} \approx$ _____.

You need to find a better estimate for $\sqrt{3}$ so you can compare it to 1.5.
Approximate $\sqrt{3}$ to the nearest hundredth.

$\sqrt{3}$ is between _____ and _____, so $\sqrt{3} \approx$ _____.

An approximate value of π is 3.14.

Plot $\sqrt{3}$, π, and 1.5 on a number line.

Read the numbers from left to right to place them in order from least to greatest.

From least to greatest, the numbers are _____, _____, _____.

Order the numbers from least to greatest.

3a. $\sqrt{5}, 2.5, \sqrt{3}$ _____

3b. $\pi^2, 10, \sqrt{75}$ _____

Approximate each irrational number to the nearest hundredth without using a calculator.

1. $\sqrt{34}$

2. $\sqrt{82}$

3. $\sqrt{45}$

4. $\sqrt{104}$

5. $\sqrt{71}$

6. $\sqrt{19}$

7. $\sqrt{24}$

8. $\sqrt{41}$

Compare. Write <, >, or =.

9. $\sqrt{3} + 2$ ⬤ $\sqrt{2} + 3$

10. $\sqrt{11} + 15$ ⬤ $\sqrt{15} + 11$

11. $\sqrt{6} + 5$ ⬤ $6 + \sqrt{5}$

12. $\sqrt{9} + 3$ ⬤ $9 + \sqrt{3}$

13. $\sqrt{15} - 3$ ⬤ $-2 + \sqrt{5}$

14. $10 - \sqrt{8}$ ⬤ $12 - \sqrt{2}$

15. $\sqrt{7} + 1$ ⬤ $\sqrt{10} - 1$

16. $\sqrt{12} + 3$ ⬤ $3 + \sqrt{11}$

Order the numbers from least to greatest.

17. $\sqrt{7}, \dfrac{\sqrt{8}}{2}, 2$

18. $\sqrt{10}, \pi, 3.5$

19. $1.5, \dfrac{\sqrt{12}}{3}, \sqrt{3}$

20. $2\sqrt{7}, \sqrt{24}, 2\pi$

Problem Solving Connections

COMMON CORE

CC.8.EE.1,
CC.8.EE.3,
CC.8.EE.4

Living on the Moon! Suppose that in the year 2050, it is possible for humans to live on the moon. The resources on the moon will allow for $\sqrt{1 \times 10^{19}}$ people to live there.

The table below gives the projected population for each of the seven continents on Earth in the year 2050.

Projected Population in 2050							
Continent	Africa	Antarctica	Asia	Australia	Europe	North America	South America
Population	2×10^9	1.0×10^3	5.43×10^9	3.09×10^7	6.03×10^8	4.38×10^8	5.36×10^8

1 Can Earth's Total Population Live on the Moon?

Could the total population of Earth live on the moon?

A Write the population of each continent using the same power of 10.

B Add the multipliers for each population. Use the same power of 10 as in **A** to write the world population.

C Write the world population in scientific notation and standard notation.

D Find the number of people who could live on the moon. Use a calculator to find $\sqrt{1 \times 10^{19}}$. Write your answer in standard notation and scientific notation.

E Can the total population of Earth live on the moon? Use your answers from parts C and D to perform a calculation and explain how the result justifies your answer.

2 Can the Population of Each Continent Live on the Moon?

The projected population of Antarctica is 1.0×10^3 people. That's just 1000 people on the continent. By comparing this population to the possible population of the moon, you can determine that the entire population of Antarctica could live on the moon. Could the entire population of each of the other continents live on the moon?

A Use subtraction with numbers in scientific notation to compare the populations of Africa, Asia, and Australia to the possible population of the moon. Explain whether the entire population of each these continents could live on the moon.

Africa:

Asia:

Australia:

>

B Use division with numbers in scientific notation to compare the populations of Europe, North America, and South America to the possible population of the moon. Explain whether the entire population of each these continents could live on the moon.

Europe:

>

North America:

>

South America:

>

C Name the continent(s) for which the entire population could live on the moon.

_____

_____

_____

3 What is the Population Density on the Moon?

Population density is a measure of the number of people per a given area. For example, the population density of Boston, Massachusettes, is about 5,000 people per square kilometer.

The land surface area of Earth is 1.4894×10^8 square kilometers. The surface area of the moon is 3.793×10^7 square kilometers. Assume that humans are able to colonize the entire surface area of the moon. If $\sqrt{1 \times 10^{19}}$ people lived on the moon, would the population density be greater on Earth or on the moon?

A Find the average population density of Earth by dividing the total population of Earth by the land surface area of Earth.

There are about _____ people per square kilometer on Earth.

B Find the average population density of the moon by dividing the possible population of the moon by the surface area of the moon.

There would be about _____ people per square kilometer on the moon.

C Use your answers from **A** and **B** to explain whether Earth or the moon would have a greater population density.

_____

_____

D **Extension** Make a conjecture about why the population density of a city like Boston is greater than the population density of Earth.

_____

_____

_____

_____

UNIT 1 TEST PREP

MULTIPLE CHOICE

1. An industrial machine creates $4^3 \cdot 4^5$ products every year. How many products does the machine create each year?

   A. 4   **C.** 64

   B. 16   **D.** 65,536

2. Simplify the expression:

$$(2^2)^4 - \left(\frac{(7-1)^9}{6^2}\right) + (20-17)^3 \times 3^8$$

   F. $2^6 - 6^{11} + 3^{11}$ **H.** $2^8 - 6^7 + 3^{11}$

   G. $4^6 - 6^{11} + 3^5$ **J.** $8^6 - 36^{11} + 9^{11}$

Use the table for 3 and 4.

Weights of Large Animals			
Animal	African Bush Elephant	Polar Bear	Ostrich
Weight (lbs)	27,000	2,000	343.92

3. What is the weight of the ostrich written scientific notation?

   A. 0.34392×10^4 pounds

   B. 3.4392×10^2 pounds

   C. 3.4392×10^3 pounds

   D. 34.392×10^4 pounds

4. How many times as great as the weight of the polar bear is the weight of the African bush elephant?

   F. 0.135×10^2 pounds

   G. 1.35×10^7 pounds

   H. 1.35×10^1 pounds

   J. 5.4×10^7 pounds

5. In 2009, the population of California was estimated as 3.696×10^7 people. The population of Florida was estimated as 1.854×10^7 people. What was the total estimated population for these two states?

   A. 5.550×10^7 people

   B. 5.550×10^5 people

   C. 1.842×10^7 people

   D. 1.842×10^1 people

6. In 2009, the population of the United States was estimated as 3.07×10^8 people. The population of Maryland was estimated as 5.7×10^6 people. About how many times greater is the population of the U.S. than the population of Maryland?

   F. 2 times

   G. 5 times

   H. 50 times

   J. 200 times

7. A square section of a kitchen floor is made of 49 square tiles. How many tiles are on each side of the square section of the kitchen floor?

   A. 4.9 tiles   **C.** 36 tiles

   B. 7 tiles   **D.** 42 tiles

8. A sculpture of a giant cube contains 1331 cubes within it. How many smaller cubes are along each edge of the sculpture?

   F. 11 cubes   **H.** 36 cubes

   G. 13 cubes   **J.** 133 cubes

9. Chen is building a birdhouse. The bottom part is a cube with a volume of $\frac{1}{8}$ cubic foot. What is the length of each edge of the cube in feet?

   A. $\frac{1}{2}$ foot

   B. $\frac{1}{3}$ foot

   C. $\frac{1}{64}$ foot

   D. $\frac{1}{512}$ foot

10. Which is approximately equal to $\sqrt{3}$?

   F. $\frac{1}{3}$

   G. 1.732050808...

   H. 3.0

   J. 9.732050808...

11. Which fraction is equivalent to $0.\overline{15}$?

   A. $\frac{1}{15}$ C. $\frac{10}{15}$

   B. $\frac{15}{99}$ D. $\frac{15}{1}$

FREE RESPONSE

12. Explain whether each of the following numbers is rational.

   $2, \frac{1}{13}, \sqrt{11}, 0.\overline{3}$

   _____

   _____

   _____

   _____

   _____

   _____

13. Find a number greater than 1 and less than 1000 that is both a perfect square and a perfect cube. Give the principal square root and the cube root of your number.

   _____

   _____

14. Explain how you know that $\sqrt{2}$ is less than $2\sqrt{2}$ without performing any calculations.

   _____

   _____

   _____

   _____

15. Explain how you know whether $\sqrt{38}$ is closer to 6 or 7 without using a calculator.

   _____

   _____

16. Give two ways to write 4^6 as a product of powers.

   _____

   _____

17. Chris needs to install carpet in a square room. The floor of the room has an area of about 876 square feet. Chris must order a whole number of square yards of carpet.

   a. About how many feet long is the room?

   _____

   _____

   b. How many square yards of carpet should Chris order? Explain your reasoning.

   _____

   _____

   _____

Functions

Unit Focus

Functions give us a way to describe relationships that happen in our lives. A function can describe the cost of a cell phone plan, predict how long it will take to drive to the beach, or help you choose the best payment plan.

In this unit, you will learn how to use a table, write a mathematical expression, or create a graph to describe the relationship between two things. You will see how each of these representations can give you important information about the relationship, and how you can use this information to make decisions.

Unit at a Glance

COMMON CORE

UNIT 2

Unpacking the Common Core State Standards

Use the table to help you understand the Common Core State Standards that are taught in this unit. Refer to the lessons listed after each standard for exploration and practice.

COMMON CORE Standards for Mathematical Content	What It Means For You
CC.8.EE.5 Graph proportional relationships, interpreting the unit rate as the slope of the graph. Compare two different proportional relationships represented in different ways. Lessons 2-2, 2-3, 2-6	You will learn how to recognize constant rates and to apply your understanding of rates to analyzing real-world situations.
CC.8.EE.6 Use similar triangles to explain why the slope m is the same between any two distinct points on a non-vertical line in the coordinate plane; **derive the equation $y = mx$ for a line through the origin and the equation $y = mx + b$ for a line intercepting the vertical axis at b.** Lesson 2-4	Equations can describe functional relationships. If you understand what the equation describes, you can use that information to understand a problem situation.
CC.8.F.1 Understand that a function is a rule that assigns to each input exactly one output. The graph of a function is the set of ordered pairs consisting of an input and the corresponding output. Lesson 2-1	A function is a special type of relationship between input values and output values. You can generate ordered pairs of input and output values in order to graph a function.
CC.8.F.2 Compare properties of two functions each represented in a different way (algebraically, graphically, numerically in tables, or by verbal descriptions). Lesson 2-6	You will learn to translate between different representations of functions such as tables, graphs, equations, and verbal descriptions.
CC.8.F.3 Interpret the equation $y = mx + b$ as defining a linear function, whose graph is a straight line; give examples of functions that are not linear. Lessons 2-2, 2-4, 2-5	The graph of a linear function is a straight line. The graph of a non-linear function is not a straight line. Every linear function can be described by a linear equation. The equation $y = mx + b$ is a linear equation in slope-intercept form.
CC.8.F.4 Construct a function to model a linear relationship between two quantities. Determine the rate of change and initial value of the function from a description of a relationship or from two (x, y) values, including reading these from a table or from a graph. Interpret the rate of change and initial value of a linear function in terms of the situation it models, and in terms of its graph or a table of values. Lessons 2-5, 2-6	You will learn to identify the slope of a line and the y-intercept using a table, graph, equation, or verbal description. The slope of a line is the rate of change of the situation modeled by a linear function. The y-intercept is the initial value of the function.

Functions, Tables, and Graphs

Essential question: *How do you represent a function with a table or graph?*

1 EXPLORE   Understanding Relationships

Carlos needs to buy some new pencils from the school supply cabinet at school. Carlos asks his classmates if they know how much pencils cost. Angela says she bought 2 pencils for $0.50. Paige bought 3 pencils for $0.75, and Spencer bought 4 pencils for $1.00.

Carlos thinks about the rule for the price of a pencil as a machine. When he puts the number of pencils he wants to buy into the machine, the machine applies a rule and tells him the total cost of that number of pencils.

Number of pencils	Rule	Cost of pencils

	Number of pencils	Rule	Cost of pencils
i.	2	?	
ii.	3	?	
iii.	4	?	
iv.	x		
v.	12		

A Use the prices in the problem to fill in rows **i–iii** of the table.

B Describe any patterns you see. Use your pattern to determine the cost of 1 pencil.

_____

_____

C Use the pattern you identified to write the rule applied by the machine. Write the rule as an algebraic expression and fill in row **iv** of the table.

D Carlos wants to buy 12 pencils. Use your rule to fill in row **v** of the table to show how much Carlos will pay for 12 pencils.

There are 6 pencil-top erasers in 2 packages of erasers. There are 9 erasers in 3 packages.

1a. Write a rule in words for the number of packages Carlos needs to buy to get *x* erasers. Then write the rule as an algebraic expression.

_____

1b. How many packages does Carlos need to buy to get 18 erasers?

_____

REFLECT

1c. How can you decide what operation to use in your rule?

_____

_____

_____

The rules in ❶ are functions, and the machines are function machines. The value that is put into a function machine is the **input**. The result after applying the function machine's rule is the **output**. A **function** is a rule that assigns exactly one output to each input.

A table of values can represent a function if each input value is paired with only one output value.

2 EXAMPLE **Recognizing Functions**

Tell whether each relationship is a function.

A

Input	Output
15	70
60	88
75	95
45	80

Each input has only one _____.

This relationship _____ a function.

B

Input	Output
14	60
13	55
14	57
15	52

The input _____ has more than one output.

This relationship _____ a function.

The input values (x) and output values (y) of a function can be displayed in a table or written as ordered pairs (x, y). These ordered pairs can be graphed in the coordinate plane to show a graph of the function.

Some function rules can be written as equations such as $y = 2x$. By substituting values for x, you can generate corresponding y-values. The ordered pairs (x, y) are solutions of the equation.

3 E X A M P L E   **Graphing a Function**

Graph the function $y = 2x + 3$.

Create a table of values.

x	$2x + 3$	y
−4	2(−4) + 3	
−1	2(☐) + 3	
0		
2		
3		

Write ordered pairs.

(x, y)
(−4, ☐)
(−1, ☐)
(0, ☐)
(☐, ☐)
(☐, ☐)

Graph the ordered pairs.

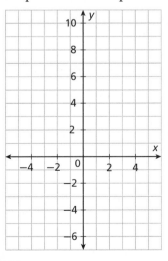

Draw a line through the points to represent all the possible x-values and their corresponding y-values.

Fill in each table. In the row with *x* as the input, write a rule as an algebraic expression for the output. Then complete the last row of the table using the rule.

1.

Input	Output
Tickets	Cost ($)
2	40
5	100
7	140
8	160
x	
10	

2.

Input	Output
Minutes	Pages Read
2	1
10	5
20	10
30	15
x	
60	

3.

Input	Output
Muffins	Cost ($)
1	2.25
3	6.75
6	13.50
12	27.00
x	
18	

Tell whether each relationship is a function.

4.

Input	6	7	8	7	9
Output	75	80	87	88	95

5.

Input	1	2	3	4	5
Output	4	8	12	16	20

_____

6. $(1, 3), (2, 5), (3, 0), (4, -1), (5, 5)$

_____

7. $(2, 7), (6, 4), (0, 3), (2, 6), (1, 5)$

_____

Graph each function on the coordinate plane.

8. $y = -2x$

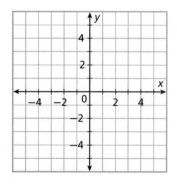

9. $y = x - 3$

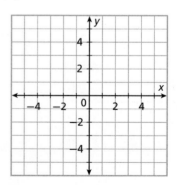

Graphing Linear Functions

Essential question: *How do you graph a linear function?*

COMMON
CORE

CC.8.EE.5
CC.8.F.3

1 **EXPLORE** Investigating Change

The U.S. Department of Agriculture defines heavy rain as rain that falls at a rate of 1.5 centimeters per hour.

A The table shows the total amount of rain that falls in various amounts of time during a heavy rain. Complete the table.

Time (h)	0	1	2	3	4	5
Total Amount of Rain (cm)	0	1.5				

B Plot the ordered pairs from the table on the coordinate plane at the right.

C How much rain falls in 3.5 hours?

_____

D Plot the point corresponding to 3.5 hours of heavy rain.

E What do you notice about all of the points you plotted?

_____

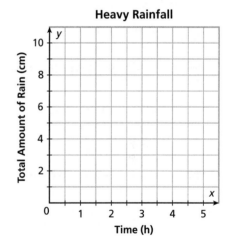

Heavy Rainfall

REFLECT

1a. Suppose you continued to plot points for times between those in the table, such as 1.2 hours or 4.5 hours. What can you say about the locations of these points?

_____

_____

1b. The U.S. Department of Agriculture defines excessive rain as rain that falls at a rate of 4 centimeters per hour. How do you think a graph of excessive rainfall would compare to the graph of heavy rainfall?

_____

_____

A **linear function** is a function whose graph is a nonvertical straight line. The function describing heavy rainfall in is a linear function because its graph is a set of points that form a straight line.

A **linear equation** is an equation that represents a linear function. The solutions of a linear equation are ordered pairs that form a straight line on the coordinate plane.

2 EXAMPLE   Graphing a Linear Equation

Experts recommend that adult dogs have a daily intake of 50 calories per kilogram of the dog's weight plus 100 calories. Write an equation that gives the recommended number of daily calories y for a dog that weighs x kilograms. Then show that the equation is a linear equation.

Write an equation.

Daily calories equals 50 times weight plus 100.

$=$ $+$

Complete the table to find some solutions of the equation.

Weight (kg), x	6	8	10	12	14
Calories, y					

Plot the points, then draw a line through the points to represent all the possible x-values and their corresponding y-values.

The equation is a linear equation because

_____

_____.

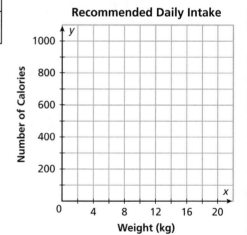

Recommended Daily Intake

TRY THIS!

2a. Graph the solutions of the linear equation $y = -2x + 1$. Then explain how the graph is different from the graph in the example.

_____

_____

The linear equation in ② has the form $y = mx + b$, where m and b are real numbers. Every equation in the form $y = mx + b$ is a linear equation. Equations that cannot be written in this form are not linear equations.

3 **EXAMPLE** Determining Whether an Equation is Linear

A square tile has a side length of x inches. The equation $y = x^2$ gives the area y of the tile in square inches. Determine whether the equation $y = x^2$ is a linear equation.

Complete the table.

Side Length, x	1	2	3	4
Area, y				

Plot the points, then draw a curve through the points to represent all the possible x-values and their corresponding y-values.

Decide whether the equation $y = x^2$ a linear equation. Explain your reasoning.

_____

_____

_____

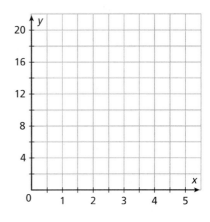

REFLECT

3a. How is the equation $y = x^2$ different from the linear equations you have graphed?

_____

3b. Explain whether you think the equation $y = 2x^2 + 4$ is a linear equation.

_____

3c. **Error Analysis** A student graphed several solutions of $y = -2x$ as shown. The student concluded that the equation is not a linear equation. Explain the student's error.

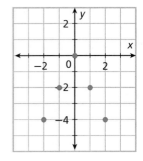

_____

_____

_____

_____

Graph solutions of each equation and tell whether the equation is linear or non-linear.

1. $y = 5 - 2x$

Input, x	−1	1	3	5
Output, y				

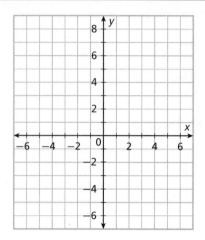

2. $y = 2 - x^2$

Input, x	−2	−1	0	1	2
Output, y					

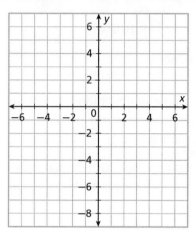

3. Olivia measured several rooms in her house in feet. She wants to express the measurements in inches. Write an equation relating feet x and inches y. Tell whether the equation is linear or linear.

4. Seth receives $100 from his grandmother for his birthday. He also saves $20 every month. Write an equation relating months x and total savings y. Tell whether the equation is linear or non-linear.

Explain whether each equation is a linear equation.

5. $y = x^2 - 1$

6. $y = 1 - x$

7. **Error Analysis** A student claims that the equation $y = 7$ is not a linear equation because it does not have the form $y = mx + b$. Do you agree or disagree? Why?

Rate of Change and Slope

Essential question: *How do you find a rate of change or a slope?*

A **rate of change** is a ratio of the amount of change in the output to the amount of change in the input.

1 **EXAMPLE** **Investigating Rates of Change**

Eve keeps a record of the number of lawns she mows and the money she earns.

	Day 1	Day 2	Day 3	Day 4	Day 5
Number of Lawns	1	3	6	8	13
Amount Earned ($)	15	45	90	120	195

Input variable: _____ Output variable: _____

Find the rates of change:

Day 1 to Day 2 $\dfrac{\text{change in \$}}{\text{change in lawns}} = \dfrac{45 - \boxed{}}{3 - 1} = \dfrac{\boxed{}}{2} = \boxed{}$

Day 2 to Day 3 $\dfrac{\text{change in \$}}{\text{change in lawns}} = \dfrac{\boxed{} - 45}{6 - \boxed{}} = \dfrac{\boxed{}}{3} = \boxed{}$

Day 3 to Day 4 $\dfrac{\text{change in \$}}{\text{change in lawns}} = \dfrac{\boxed{} - \boxed{}}{\boxed{} - 6} = \dfrac{\boxed{}}{2} = \boxed{}$

Day 4 to Day 5 $\dfrac{\text{change in \$}}{\text{change in lawns}} = \dfrac{\boxed{} - \boxed{}}{\boxed{} - \boxed{}} = \dfrac{\boxed{}}{\boxed{}} = \boxed{}$

The rates of change are constant / variable.

TRY THIS!

1. The table shows the approximate height of a football after it is kicked.

Time (s)	0	0.5	1.5	2
Height (ft)	0	18	31	26

Input variable: _____ Output variable: _____

Find the rates of change:

The rates of change are constant / variable.

You can also use a graph to find rates of change.

2 EXPLORE Using Graphs to Find Rates of Change

**The graph shows the distance Nathan bicycled over time.
What is Nathan's rate of change?**

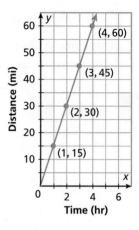

A Find the rate of change from 1 hour to 2 hours.

$$\frac{\text{change in distance}}{\text{change in hours}} = \frac{30 - \boxed{}}{2 - 1} = \frac{\boxed{}}{1} = \boxed{} \text{ miles per hour}$$

B Find the rate of change from 1 hour to 4 hours.

$$\frac{\text{change in distance}}{\text{change in hours}} = \frac{60 - \boxed{}}{4 - \boxed{}} = \frac{\boxed{}}{\boxed{}} = \boxed{} \text{ miles per hour}$$

C Recall that the graph of a proportional relationship is a straight line through the origin. Explain whether the relationship between Nathan's time and distance appears to be a proportional relationship.

_____

_____

D Find Nathan's unit rate.

_____

E Compare the rate of change to the unit rate.

_____

REFLECT

2a. Does it matter what interval you use when you find the rate of change of a proportional relationship? Explain.

_____

_____

2b. **Conjecture** Do you think that the value of r in the point $(1, r)$ is always the unit rate for any situation? Explain.

_____

_____

_____

When the rate of change of a relationship or function is constant, every segment of its graph has the same steepness and together they form a straight line. The constant rate of change is called the *slope* of the line.

The **slope** of a line is the ratio of the change in *y*-values (rise) for a segment of the graph to the corresponding change in *x*-values (run).

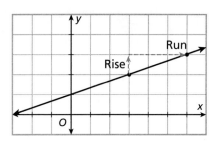

3 EXAMPLE   Calculating Slope

Find the slope of the line.

A

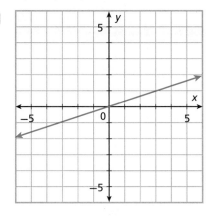

$$\text{slope} = \frac{\text{rise}}{\text{run}}$$

$$= \frac{\quad}{\quad}$$

B

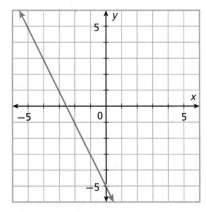

$$\text{slope} = \frac{\text{rise}}{\text{run}}$$

$$= \frac{\quad}{\quad} = \quad$$

REFLECT

3a. If a line rises from left to right, what is the sign of its slope? If a line falls from left to right, what is the sign of its slope?

_____

3b. What type of line has a slope equal to 0?

_____

3c. What happens when you try to calculate the slope of a vertical line?

_____

PRACTICE

1. Gerri dropped a ball from the top of a building. Use the table to find the rate of change over each interval.

Time (s)	0	1	2	3	4
Height of Ball (ft)	256	240	192	112	0

    a. 0 seconds to 1 second   _____

    b. 3 seconds to 4 seconds   _____

    c. 1 second to 3 seconds   _____

2. Is the ball's rate of change constant or variable?

_____

Use the graph to find the average rate of change over each interval.

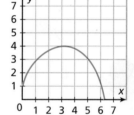

3. $x = 0$ to $x = 3$

_____

4. $x = 5$ to $x = 6$

_____

Erica walks to her friend Philip's house at a constant pace. The graph shows Erica's distance from home over time.

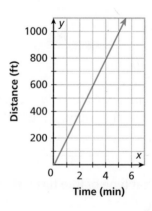

5. Without calculating slope, tell whether the slope is positive or negative.

_____

6. Find the slope of the line.

_____

7. Does the value of r in the point $(1, r)$ correspond to Erica's unit rate? Explain.

_____

Slope-Intercept Form

COMMON
CORE

CC.8.EE.6
CC.8.F.3

Essential question: *How can you derive the slope-intercept form of a line?*

The graph of every non-vertical line crosses the *y*-axis. The **y-intercept** is the *y*-coordinate of the point where the graph intersects the *y*-axis. The *x*-coordinate of this point is always 0.

To write the equation of a line or to graph a line, you just need to know its slope and *y*-intercept.

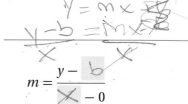

1 EXPLORE   Deriving the Slope-Intercept Formula

A Let *L* be a line with slope *m* and *y*-intercept *b*. Circle the point that must be on the line. Justify your choice. $\times, y$

(*b*, 0)   (0, *b*)   (0, *m*)   (*m*, 0)

Let (*x*, *y*) be a point on line *L* other than the point containing the *y*-intercept.

B Write an expression for the change in *y* values between the point that includes the *y*-intercept and the point (*x*, *y*). _____

C Write an expression for the change in *x* values between the point that includes the *y*-intercept and the point (*x*, *y*). $y = mx$ $y - b = mx$

D Recall that slope is the ratio of change in *y* to change in *x*. Complete the equation for the slope *m* of the line.
$$m = \frac{y - b}{x - 0}$$

E In an equation of a line, we often want *y* by itself on one side of the equation. Solve the equation from **D** for *y*.

$y = mx + b$

$$m = \frac{y - b}{x}$$ *Simplify the denominator.*

$y - b = mx$

$$m \cdot x = \frac{y - b}{x} \cdot x$$ *Multiply both sides of the equation by x.*

$\dfrac{y - b}{x} = m$

$mx = y - b$

$mx + b = y - b + b$ *Add _____ to both sides of the equation.*

$mx + b = y$

$y = mx + b$ *Write the equation with y on the left side.*

REFLECT

1. Write the equation of a line with slope *m* that passes through the origin.

_____

The equation $y = mx + b$ is called the **slope-intercept form** of the equation of a line. In this form, it is easy to see the slope and the y-intercept. When the equation of a line is in slope-intercept form, you can quickly graph the line.

2 EXAMPLE   Using Slope-Intercept Form to Graph a Line

Graph $y = -2x + 5$.

Step 1 Identify the slope and the y-intercept.

slope: $m = \boxed{} = \dfrac{\boxed{}}{1}$

y-intercept: $b = \boxed{}$

Step 2 The point that contains the y-intercept is $\left(0, \boxed{}\right)$. Plot this point.

Step 3 Use the slope to find a second point on the line. Count down _____ unit(s) and right _____ unit(s). Plot this point.

Step 4 Draw a line connecting the two points.

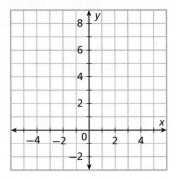

TRY THIS!

Write an equation for the line with the given slope and y-intercept.

1. slope: -4; y-intercept: 6

_____

2. slope: $\frac{5}{2}$; y-intercept: -3

_____

Graph each equation.

3. $y = \frac{1}{2}x + 1$

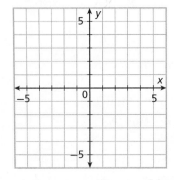

4. $y = -3x + 4$

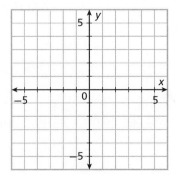

Writing Equations to Describe Functions

COMMON
CORE

Essential question: *How do you write an equation for a function given a table, graph, or description?*

CC.8.F.3
CC.8.F.4

1. EXPLORE Writing an Equation for a Function from a Table

Elizabeth can choose from several monthly cell phone plans. The cost of each plan is a linear function of the number of minutes that are included in the plan. Write an equation in slope-intercept form that represents the function.

Minutes Included, x	100	200	300	400	500
Cost of Plan ($), y	18	28	38	48	58

A Choose any two ordered pairs from the table to find the slope.

$$m = \frac{y_2 - y_1}{x_2 - x_1} = \frac{\boxed{} - \boxed{}}{\boxed{} - \boxed{}} = \frac{\boxed{}}{\boxed{}} = \boxed{}$$

B Use the equation $y = mx + b$ and any point from the table.
Substitute values for y, m, and x into the equation and solve for b.

$$y = mx + b$$

$$\boxed{} = \boxed{} \cdot \boxed{} + b \quad \text{Substitute for y, m, and x.}$$

$$\boxed{} = \boxed{} + b \quad \text{Simplify on the right side.}$$

$$\frac{-\boxed{} \quad -\boxed{}}{} \quad \quad \begin{array}{l}\text{Subtract the number that is added}\\ \text{to b from both sides.}\end{array}$$

$$\boxed{} = b$$

C Use the slope and y-intercept values to write an equation in slope-intercept form.

$$y = \boxed{} x + \boxed{}$$

REFLECT

1a. Use the equation to predict the cost of a cell phone plan that includes 175 minutes.

_____

1b. What is the base price for any cell phone plan, regardless of how many minutes are included?

_____

1c. **What If?** Elizabeth's cell phone company changed the prices for each of their plans. Write an equation in slope-intercept form that represents the function.

Minutes Included, x	100	200	300	400	500
Cost of Plan ($), y	30	35	40	45	50

_____

2 EXPLORE   Writing an Equation for a Function from a Graph

Kate is planning a trip to the beach. She used an estimated average speed to make a graph showing the progress she expects to make on her trip. Write an equation in slope-intercept form that represents the function.

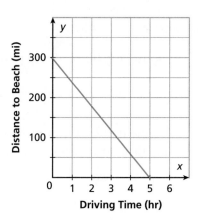

A Choose two points on the graph to find the slope.

$$m = \frac{y_2 - y_1}{x_2 - x_1} = \frac{\boxed{} - \boxed{}}{\boxed{} - \boxed{}} = \frac{\boxed{}}{\boxed{}} = \boxed{}$$

B Read the y-intercept from the graph.

$b = \boxed{}$

C Use your slope and y-intercept values to write an equation in slope-intercept form.

_____

2a. What does the value of the slope represent in this context?

_____

_____

2b. Is the slope positive or negative? What does the sign of the slope mean in this context?

_____

_____

2c. Describe the meaning of the y-intercept.

_____

_____

The rate at which crickets chirp is a linear function of temperature. At 59 °F, they chirp 76 times per minute, and at 65 °F, they chirp 100 times per minute. Write an equation in slope-intercept form that represents the function.

A Identify the input and output variables in this relationship.

Input variable: _____   Output variable: _____

B Write the information given in the problem as ordered pairs.

At 59 °F, crickets chirp 76 times per minute: (___ , ___)

At 65 °F, crickets chirp 100 times per minute: (___ , ___)

C Find the slope.

$$m = \frac{y_2 - y_1}{x_2 - x_1} = \frac{\boxed{} - \boxed{}}{\boxed{} - \boxed{}} = \frac{\boxed{}}{\boxed{}} = \boxed{}$$

D Use the equation $y = mx + b$ and one of the ordered pairs. Substitute values for y, m, and x into the equation and solve for b.

$$y = mx + b$$

$\boxed{} = \boxed{} \cdot \boxed{} + b$ *Substitute for y, m, and x.*

$\boxed{} = \boxed{} + b$ *Simplify on the right side.*

$\dfrac{-\boxed{} \quad -\boxed{}}{}$ *Subtract the number that is added to b from both sides.*

$\boxed{} = b$

E Write an equation in slope-intercept form.

_____

REFLECT

3a. Predict the number of chirps per minute when the temperature is 72 °F.

_____

3b. Without graphing, tell whether the graph of this function rises or falls from left to right. What does the sign of the slope mean in this context?

_____

_____

_____

The table shows the temperature at different altitudes. The temperature is a linear function of the altitude.

Altitude (ft), x	0	2,000	4,000	6,000	8,000	10,000	12,000
Temperature (°F), y	59	51	43	35	27	19	11

1. Find the slope of the function.

2. Find the y-intercept of the function.

3. Write an equation in slope-intercept form that represents the function.

4. Use your equation to determine the temperature at an altitude of 5,000 feet.

The graph shows a scuba diver's ascent over time.

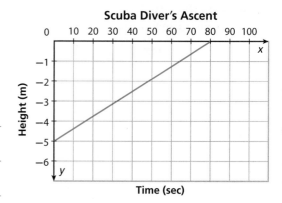

Scuba Diver's Ascent

5. Use the graph to find the slope of the line. Tell what the slope means in this context.

6. Identify the y-intercept. Tell what the y-intercept means in this context.

7. Write an equation in slope-intercept form that represents the function.

The formula for converting Celsius temperatures to Fahrenheit temperatures is a linear function. Water freezes at 0 °C, or 32 °F, and it boils at 100 °C, or 212 °F.

8. Find the slope and y-intercept. Then write an equation in slope-intercept form that represents the function.

9. Average human body temperature is 37 °C. What is this temperature in degrees Fahrenheit?

Comparing Functions

COMMON
CORE

CC.8.EE.5
CC.8.F.2
CC.8.F.4

Essential question: *How can you use tables, graphs, and equations to compare functions?*

1 EXPLORE · Comparing a Table and a Graph

The table and graph show how many words Morgan and Brian typed correctly on a typing test. For both students, the relationship between words typed correctly and time is linear.

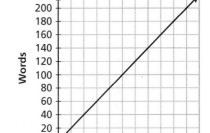

Brian's Typing Test

Morgan's Typing Test					
Time (min)	2	4	6	8	10
Words	30	60	90	120	150

A Find Morgan's unit rate.

_____

B Find Brian's unit rate.

_____

C Which student types more correct words per minute?

_____

REFLECT

1a. Sketch a graph of Morgan's test results on the same coordinate grid as Brian's results. How are the graphs similar? How are they different?

_____

_____

1b. Katie types 17 correct words per minute. Explain how a graph of Katie's test results would compare to Morgan's and Brian's.

_____

_____

1c. The equation that describes Jen's test results is $y = 24x$. Explain how a graph of Jen's test results would compare to Morgan's and Brian's.

_____

_____

Josh and Maggie buy MP3 files from different music download services. With both services, the monthly charge is a linear function of the number of songs downloaded. The cost at Josh's service is described by $y = 0.50x + 10$ where y is the cost in dollars and x is the number of songs downloaded.

Cost of MP3s at Maggie's Music Service					
Songs, x	5	10	15	20	25
Cost ($), y	4.95	9.90	14.85	19.80	24.75

A Find the unit rate of each function.

Josh: _____   Maggie: _____

B Which function has the greater rate of change? What does that mean in this context?

_____

C Write an equation in slope-intercept form to describe the cost at Maggie's music service.

$y = mx + b$

[ ] = [ ] · [ ] $+ b$ *Substitute for y, m, and b.*

[ ] = [ ] $+ b$ *Subtract the number that is added to b from both sides.*

$-$ [ ] $-$ [ ]
_____

[ ] = b

$y =$ [ ] $x +$ [ ]

D Describe each service's cost in words using the meanings of the slopes and y-intercepts.

_____

_____

REFLECT

2a. How much does it cost at each service to download 20 songs?

_____

2b. You are trying to choose between these two music services. How could you decide which service is better for you?

_____

_____

Jamal wants to buy a new game system that costs $200. He only has $100 today, so he compares layaway plans at different stores.

The plan at Store A is shown on the graph.

Store B requires an initial payment of $60 and weekly payments of $20 until the balance is paid in full.

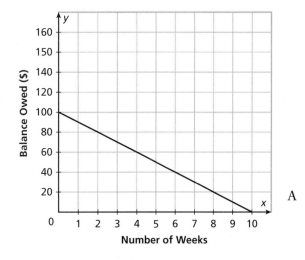

A Use the graph of the layaway plan at Store A to write an equation in slope-intercept form. Let *x* represent number of weeks and *y* represent balance owed.

_____

B Use the description of the layaway plan at Store B to write an equation in slope-intercept form. Let *x* represent number of weeks and *y* represent balance owed.

_____

C Sketch a graph of the plan at Store B on the same grid as Store A.

D How can you use the graphs to tell which plan requires the greater down payment? How can you use the equations?

_____

_____

_____

E How can you use the graphs to tell which plan requires the greater weekly payment? How can you use the equations?

_____

_____

F Which plan allows Jamal to pay for the game system faster? Explain.

_____

_____

The table and the graph display two different linear functions.

Input, x	Output, y
−3	5
−1	1
2	−5
3	−7
6	−13

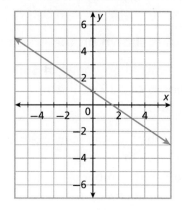

1. Find the slope of each function.

   Table: _____   Graph: _____

2. Without graphing the function represented in the table, tell which function's graph is steeper.

   _____

   _____

3. Write an equation for each function.

   Table: _____   Graph: _____

4. Use the equations from **3** to tell which function has the greater y-intercept.

   _____

Aisha runs a tutoring business. Students may choose to pay $15 per hour or they may follow the plan shown on the graph.

5. Describe the plan shown on the graph.

   _____

6. Sketch a graph showing the $15 per hour option.

7. What does the intersection of the two graphs mean?

   _____

8. If you wanted to hire Aisha for tutoring, how can you decide which payment option is better for you?

   _____

   _____

Analyzing Graphs

Essential question: *How can you describe a relationship given a graph and sketch a graph given a description?*

1 EXPLORE   Interpreting Graphs

A roller coaster park is open from May to October each year. The graph shows the number of park visitors over its season.

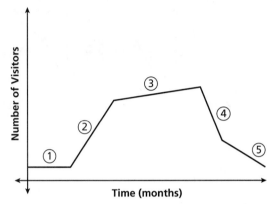

A Segment 1 shows that attendance during the opening days of the park's season stayed constant. Describe what Segment 2 shows.

_____

_____

B Based on the time frame, give a possible explanation for the change in attendance represented by Segment 2.

_____

_____

C Which segments of the graph show decreasing attendance? Give a possible explanation.

_____

_____

REFLECT

1. Explain how the slope of each segment of the graph is related to whether attendance increases or decreases.

_____

_____

Grace, Jet, and Mike are studying 100 words for a spelling bee.

- **Grace started by learning many words each day, but then learned fewer and fewer words each day.**

- **Jet learned the same number of words each day.**

- **Mike started by learning only a few words each day, but then learned a greater number of words each day.**

Match each student's study progress with the correct graph.

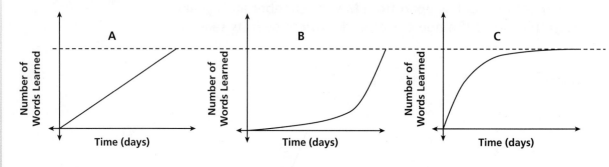

A   Describe the progress represented by Graph A.

_____

_____

_____

B   Describe the progress represented by Graph B.

_____

_____

_____

C   Describe the progress represented by Graph C.

_____

_____

_____

D   Determine which graph represents each student's study progress and write the students' names under the appropriate graphs.

REFLECT

2.   What would it mean if one of the graphs slanted downward from left to right?

_____

_____

Mrs. Sutton provides free math tutoring to her students every day after school. No one comes to tutoring sessions during the first week of school. Over the next two weeks, use of the tutoring service gradually increases.

A   Sketch a graph showing the number of students who use the tutoring service over the first three weeks of school.

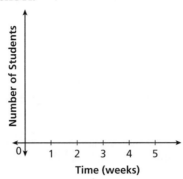

B   Mrs. Sutton's students are told that they will have a math test at the end of the fifth week of school. How do you think this will affect the number of students who come to tutoring?

_____

_____

C   Considering your answer to B , sketch a graph showing the number of students who might use the tutoring service over the first six weeks of school.

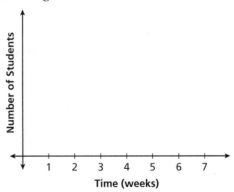

3a. Suppose Mrs. Sutton offered bonus credit to students who came to tutoring sessions. How do you think this would affect the number of students who come to tutoring?

_____

_____

3b. How would your answer to **3a** affect the graph?

_____

_____

In a lab environment, colonies of bacteria follow a predictable pattern of growth. The graph shows this growth over time.

1. During which phase is growth slowest? During which phase is growth fastest? Explain.

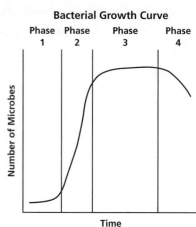

Bacterial Growth Curve

_____

_____

_____

_____

2. What is happening to the population during Phase 3?

_____

_____

_____

3. What is happening to the population during Phase 4?

_____

_____

A woodland area on an island contains a population of foxes. The graph describes the changes in the fox population over time.

4. What is happening to the fox population before time *t*?

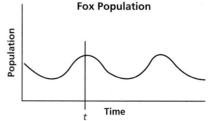

Fox Population

_____

_____

5. At time *t*, a conservation organization moves a large group of foxes to the island. Sketch a graph to show how this action might affect the population on the island after time *t*.

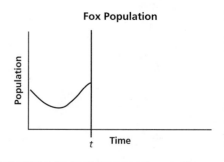

Fox Population

6. At some point after time *t*, a forest fire destroys part of the woodland area on the island. Describe how your graph from problem **5** might change.

_____

_____

_____

Problem Solving Connections

COMMON CORE

CC.8.EE.5; CC.8.EE.6
CC.8.F.1; CC.8.F.3
CC.8.F.4; CC.8.F.5

Does Staying in School Pay? Will's parents tell him that the key to success is a good education. Attending college or trade school after earning a high school diploma may introduce Will to new and interesting ideas, but will post-high school education translate into financial success?

1 Find Rates of Change

The table shows the median starting salaries for people who have received a high school diploma and people who have completed additional years of school at the university Will's parents want him to attend.

Years of School After High School	0	2	4	6
Median Starting Salary ($)	29,000	41,000	53,000	65,000

A What is the median starting salary for someone with only a high school diploma?

_____

What is the median starting salary for someone who completed four years at the university?

_____

B Find the rate of change for each two-year period shown in the table. Is the rate of change for this data constant or variable?

What is the unit rate? Explain what the unit rate means in this context.

2 Graph the Data and Write an Equation

A Plot the points from the table on the coordinate grid. Sketch a graph of the function.

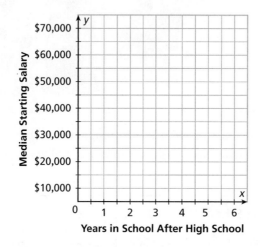

Years in School After High School

B Does the graph look like you expected? Why or why not?

_____

_____

C What is the slope of the line? _____

What is the y-intercept of the function? _____

Write an equation in slope-intercept form that describes the line.

_____

D Use your equation to predict the median starting salary for someone who completes five years at the university.

E Use your equation to predict how many years of school after high school Will would need to complete in ordered to expect a starting salary of about $100,000.

F Explain whether you think you could use the equation to determine how many years of post-high school education would translate into a starting salary of $1,000,000.

_____

_____

_____

3 Analyze Data

A Another study reports that the median starting salary for people with high school diplomas is $32,000. This study still reports that each additional year of education yields an additional $6,000 in starting salary. Sketch a graph of the results from this study. How is the graph different from your original graph?

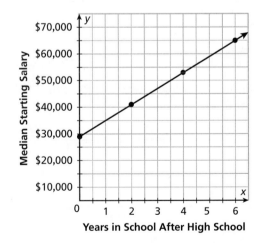

_____

B How would the original graph change if starting salaries for high school graduates began at $29,000, but each additional year of education translated to an additional $8,000 in starting salary?

_____

4 Answer the Question

A Do you agree with Will's parents? Do years in school translate into financial success? Explain.

_____

_____

_____

_____

_____

_____

_____

_____

Extend the Ideas

B Assume that a typical adult will work for 45 years before retiring. Do you think you could accurately predict a person's lifetime earnings while they were employed using the information in this activity? Justify your answer.

_____

_____

_____

_____

_____

_____

C Use the internet, almanacs, magazines, or newspapers to research starting salaries for different fields of work.

_____

_____

_____

_____

_____

_____

Name _____ Class _____ Date _____

MULTIPLE CHOICE

1. Bill keeps track of his study time and test results.

Study Time (hr)	2	4	3	?
Score	80	95	88	82

Which number would complete the table so that the relationship is a function?

A. 1

B. 2

C. 3

D. 4

2. Which table displays a non-linear function?

F.

Input	1	2	3	4
Output	−2	−1	0	1

G.

Input	1	2	3	4
Output	3	6	9	12

H.

Input	1	2	3	4
Output	1	4	9	16

J.

Input	1	2	3	4
Output	5	7	9	11

3. The graph shows Elisabeth's progress as she reads. Find her unit rate.

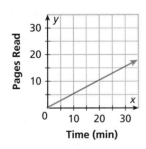

A. $\frac{1}{2}$ page per minute

B. 1 page per minute

C. $1\frac{1}{2}$ pages per minute

D. 2 pages per minute

4. Marco has a paper route. He is paid $15 each week and $0.10 for each paper he delivers. Which equation shows the relationship between the number of papers he delivers and his total income for one week?

F. $y = 15x + 0.10$

G. $y = 15x + 15$

H. $y = 0.10x + 0.10$

J. $y = 0.10x + 15$

5. Nayaleh is raising money for her school by selling candy. The amount of money y that she needs to reach her sales goal depends on the number of bags x that she sells. This is represented by the equation $y = 100 - 5x$. What does 100 represent in the equation?

A. Price of each bag of candy

B. Nayaleh's sales goal

C. Number of bags sold

D. Number of bags to sell

6. A café pays its servers a salary plus commission for selling certain items. The servers are paid different rates based on their length of employment. Which server earns the highest commission per item?

F.

Qualifying Items	2	4	6	8
Total Earned	148	156	164	172

G.

Qualifying Items	2	4	6	8
Total Earned	134	138	142	146

H.

Qualifying Items	2	4	6	8
Total Earned	130	140	150	160

J.

Qualifying Items	2	4	6	8
Total Earned	136	142	148	154

7. Which equation describes the function?

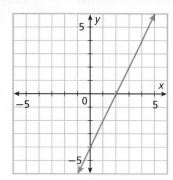

A. $y = 2x - 4$ **C.** $y = 4 - 2x$

B. $y = 4x - 2$ **D.** $y = 2 - 4x$

FREE RESPONSE

Ryan runs a frozen yogurt stand at a farmers' market. The graph shows how Ryan adjusts his sales price throughout the year, depending on his expected sales.

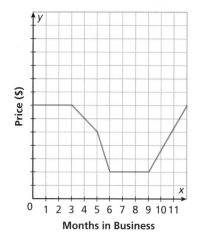

Months in Business

8. Which period do you think represents the winter months? Justify your answer.

_____

_____

_____

9. Between which months does the graph increase?

_____

10. On August 9, 2007, the bald eagle was removed from the federal list of endangered species. The table shows the growth in the bald eagle population. Explain whether the population growth is linear.

Year	1974	1984	1995	2005
Breeding Pairs of Eagles	791	2238	4712	7066

_____

_____

11. Train 1 leaves the station, and at time t, its distance from the station is $d = 65t$. Train 2's distance from the station is recorded in the table. Which train is traveling at the faster speed?

Time (hr)	1	3	6	10
Distance from Station (mi)	75	225	450	750

_____

_____

_____

Blake is driving to Washington, D.C. He recorded his progress in a table.

Time (hrs)	2	5	7	11
Distance to D.C. (mi)	860	665	535	275

12. What is Blake's average speed?

_____

_____

13. How far away from D.C. was Blake when he started his trip?

_____

_____

_____

_____

Equations

Unit Focus

Equations are used to model situations and relationships. They can help you answer questions about a situation. Some situations require more than one equation to completely describe all the relationships in the context. Many of these situations can be described by a system of equations in two variables. Solving a system of equations means finding values for each variable that make all the equations in the system true.

Unit at a Glance

COMMON CORE

Lesson	Standards for Mathematical Content
3-1 Solving Equations	CC.8.EE.7b
3-2 Analyzing Solutions	CC.8.EE.7a
3-3 Solving Systems Graphically	CC.8.EE.8a, CC.8.EE.8c
3-4 Solving Systems Algebraically	CC.8.EE.8b, CC.8.EE.8c
Problem Solving Connections	
Test Prep	

Unpacking the Common Core State Standards

Use the table to help you understand the Common Core State Standards that are taught in this unit. Refer to the lessons listed after each standard for exploration and practice.

COMMON CORE Standards for Mathematical Content	What It Means For You
CC.8.EE.7a Give examples of linear equations in one variable with one solution, infinitely many solutions, or no solutions. Show which of these possibilities is the case by successively transforming the given equation into simpler forms, until an equivalent equation of the form $x = a$, $a = a$, or $a = b$ results (where a and b are different numbers). Lesson 3-2	Some equations have only one solution. Other equations have so many solutions that you can't count them all. Other equations have no solution. You will learn to recognize how many solutions a particular equation has.
CC.8.EE.7b Solve linear equations with rational number coefficients, including equations whose solutions require expanding expressions using the distributive property and collecting like terms. Lesson 3-1	Simple one-step equations can be solved by applying only one property of equality. Other equations may require you to perform operations with fractions, decimals, or integers, to apply more than one property of equality, or to use other properties of operations, such as the distributive property.
CC.8.EE.8a Understand that solutions to a system of two linear equations in two variables correspond to points of intersection of their graphs, because points of intersection satisfy both equations simultaneously. Lesson 3-3	When you graph the solutions of a linear equation in two variables, the points fall on a line. To solve a system of two equations by graphing, you graph the solutions of each equation in the system. If a point lies on both lines at the same time (the lines intersect at one or more points), then that point is a solution of both equations.
CC.8.EE.8b Solve systems of two linear equations in two variables algebraically, and estimate solutions by graphing the equations. Solve simple cases by inspection. Lesson 3-4	Sometimes it is difficult to identify the solution of a system of equations by graphing. You can use graphing to estimate the solution, but you will need to use algebraic methods to solve the system.
CC.8.EE.8c Solve real-world and mathematical problems leading to two linear equations in two variables. Lessons 3-3, 3-4	Many real-world problems can be solved by writing and solving a system of linear equations. Learning to write and solve systems of equations will allow you to solve these kinds of problems.

Solving Equations

Essential question: *How do you solve equations by combining like terms and multiplying expressions?*

COMMON CORE

CC.8.EE.7b

1 EXPLORE   Solving Equations by Combining Like Terms

A soccer club spent $97.50 on trophies from a custom trophy company. The cost of manufacturing x custom trophies is $18.50 for the setup cost, plus $12.50 per trophy. To ship the trophies, the company charges a standard fee of $4 per order plus $2.50 per trophy. How many trophies did the soccer club order?

A Write an expression representing the **cost of manufacturing**.

Setup cost   +   Cost for x trophies

[   ]   + $12.50x$

B Write an expression representing the **cost of shipping**.

Standard fee + Cost for x trophies

[   ]   +   [   ]

C Write an equation that can be solved to find the number of trophies the soccer club ordered.

Cost of manufacturing   +   Cost of shipping   =   Club's total cost

[   ]   +   [   ]   =   [   ]

D Solve your equation for x.

The soccer club ordered _____ trophies.

TRY THIS!

Solve each equation.

1a. $14x + 6 - 10x + 30 = 64$

1b. $2\frac{1}{3}x + 10 + 5\frac{2}{3}x - 9\frac{1}{2} = 12\frac{1}{2}$

Carla chose a number between 1 and 50 and then described to Henry how he could determine the number she chose.

Carla says, "If you subtract 5 from my number, multiply that quantity by 4, and then add 7 to the result, you get 35."

Write an equation that Henry can solve to find Carla's number.

A First write an expression for "subtract 5 from my number."

_____

B Use your answer to **A** to write an expression for "multiply that quantity by 4."

_____

C Now use your answer to **B** to write an expression for "then add 7 to the result."

_____

D Use your answer to **C** and the rest of Carla's description to write an equation that you can solve to find Carla's number.

_____

E Solve the equation for x. Use the Distributive Property to simplify one side of the equation before combining like terms.

Carla's number is _____.

TRY THIS!

Solve each equation.

2a. $3(x + 2) + 4 = 31$

2b. $4 - 3(x + 2) - 2(x - 4) + 8 = -1$

At Silver Gym, membership is $25 per month, and personal training sessions are $30 each. At Fit Factor, membership is $65 per month, and personal training sessions are $20 each. In one month, how many personal training sessions would Sarah have to buy to make the total cost at the two gyms equal?

A Write an expression representing the **total monthly cost at Silver Gym**.

Monthly membership	+	Cost for x training sessions
	+	$30x$

B Write an expression representing the **total monthly cost at Fit Factor**.

Monthly membership	+	Cost for x training sessions
	+	

C How can you find the number of personal training sessions in one month that would make the total costs of the gyms equal?

_____

D Write an equation that can be solved to find the number of training sessions in one month that makes the total costs equal.

Total cost at Silver Gym	=	Total cost at Fit Factor
	=	

E Solve the equation for x. Use inverse operations to get all variable terms on one side of the equation and all constants on the other side.

Sarah would have to buy _____ personal training sessions to make the total cost at the two gyms equal.

TRY THIS!

Solve each equation.

3a. $10x + 5 = 20 - 20x$

3b. $\frac{1}{4}x + 4 = \frac{3}{4}x - 8$

Solve each equation.

1. $3x + 4 + 2x + 5 = 34$

2. $2.5x - 5 + 3x + 8 = 19.5$

3. $\frac{1}{2}x + 6 - 2x + \frac{1}{2} = \frac{7}{2}$

4. $-10x - 3 - 2.5x + 20 = 67$

5. $2(x + 1) + 4 = 12$

6. $-3(x + 4) + 15 = -12$

7. $15 - 3(x - 1) = 12$

8. $3(x - 2) + 2(x + 1) = -14$

9. $\frac{1}{2}(x + 8) - 15 = -3$

10. $2.5(x + 2) + 4.5 + 1.5(x - 3) = 15$

The monthly membership dues and private lesson fees at three tennis clubs are shown in the table.

	Club A	Club B	Club C
Monthly Membership Dues	$25	$55	$15
Private Lesson Fee	$30	$20	$40

11. After how many private lessons in one month is the total monthly cost of Club A equal to the total monthly cost at Club B?

12. After how many private lessons in one month is the total monthly cost of Club A equal to the total monthly cost at Club C?

13. After how many private lessons in one month is the total monthly cost of Club B equal to the total monthly cost at Club C?

Analyzing Solutions

3-2

Essential question: *How can you give examples of equations with a given number of solutions?*

COMMON CORE

CC.8.EE.7a

So far, when you solved a linear equation in one variable, you found one value of x that makes the equation a true statement. When you simplify some equations, you may find that they do not have one solution.

1 EXPLORE Determining the Number of Solutions

Use the properties of equality to simplify each equation. Tell whether the final equation is a true statement.

A $4x - 3 = 2x + 13$

$$4x - 3 = \quad 2x + 13$$

$$\underline{\quad} \quad \underline{\quad}$$

$$\boxed{\ } = 2x + \boxed{\ }$$

$$\underline{\boxed{\ }} \quad \underline{\boxed{\ }}$$

$$2x = 16$$

$$\frac{2x}{\boxed{\ }} = \frac{16}{\boxed{\ }}$$

$$x = \boxed{\ }$$

The statement is true / false.

B $4x - 5 = 2(2x - 1) - 3$

$$4x - 5 = 2(2x - 1) - 3$$

$$4x - 5 = \boxed{\ }x - \boxed{\ } - 3$$

$$4x - 5 = 4x - \boxed{\ }$$

$$\underline{\boxed{\ }} \quad \underline{\boxed{\ }}$$

$$-5 = \boxed{\ }$$

The statement is true / false.

C $4x + 2 = 4x - 5$

$$4x + 2 = 4x - 5$$

$$\underline{\boxed{\ }} \quad \underline{\boxed{\ }}$$

$$4x = \quad 4x - 7$$

$$\underline{\boxed{\ }} \quad \underline{\boxed{\ }}$$

$$\boxed{\ } = \boxed{\ }$$

The statement is true / false.

REFLECT

1a. What happens when you substitute any value for x in the original equation in **B**? In the original equation in **C**?

_____

_____

_____

When you simplify an equation using the properties of equality, you will find one of three results.

Result	What does this mean?	How many solutions?
$x = a$	When the value of x is a, the equation is a true statement.	1
$a = a$	Any value of x makes the equation a true statement.	Infinitely many
$a = b$	There is no value of x that makes the equation a true statement.	0

2 EXPLORE — Writing Equations with a Given Number of Solutions

Write a linear equation in one variable that has no solutions.

You can use the strategy of working backward:

A Start with a false statement such as $3 = 5$. Add the same variable term to both sides.

_____

B Next, add the same constant to both sides and combine like terms on each side of the equation.

_____

C Verify that your equation has no solutions by using properties of equality to simplify your equation.

REFLECT

2a. Explain why the result of the process above is an equation with no solutions.

_____

_____

_____

TRY THIS!

Tell whether each equation has one, zero, or infinitely many solutions.

1. $6 + 3x = x - 8$ **2.** $8x + 4 = 4(2x + 1)$

Complete each equation so that it has the indicated number of solutions.

3. No solutions: $3x + 1 = 3x + \boxed{}$ **4.** Infinitely many: $2x - 4 = 2x - \boxed{}$

Solving Systems Graphically

Essential question: *How can you solve a system of equations by graphing?*

CC.8.EE.8a
CC.8.EE.8c

1 **E X P L O R E** **Investigating Systems of Equations**

A Graph the system of linear functions: $\begin{cases} y = 3x - 2 \\ y = -2x + 3 \end{cases}$.

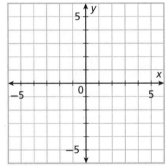

B Explain how to tell whether the ordered pair $(2, -1)$ is a solution of the equation $y = 3x - 2$ without using the graph.

_____

_____

C Explain how to tell whether the ordered pair $(2, -1)$ is a solution of the equation $y = -2x + 3$ without using the graph.

_____

_____

D Explain how to use the graph to tell whether the ordered pair $(2, -1)$ is a solution of either equation.

_____

_____

E Find an ordered pair that is a solution of both equations. Test the coordinates in each equation to verify your hypothesis.

The point _____ is a solution of both equations.

ordered pair (x, y) is a solution of an equation in two variables if substituting the x- and y-values into the equation results in a true statement. A **system of equations** is a set of equations that have the same variables. An ordered pair is a solution of a system of equations if it is a solution of every equation in the system.

Since the graph of a function represents all ordered pairs that are solutions of the related equation, if a point lies on the graphs of two functions, the point is a solution of both related equations.

2 EXAMPLE   Solving Systems Graphically

Solve each system by graphing.

A $\begin{cases} y = -x + 4 \\ y = 3x \end{cases}$

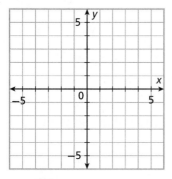

Start by graphing each function.

Identify if there are any ordered pairs that are solutions of both equations.

The solution of the system appears to be

_____.

To check your answer, you can substitute the values for x and y into each equation and make sure the equations are true statements.

B $\begin{cases} y = 2x - 2 \\ y = 2x + 4 \end{cases}$

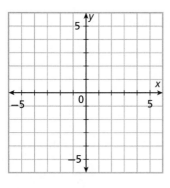

Start by graphing each function.

Identify if there are any ordered pairs that are solutions of both equations.

The graphs are parallel, so there is no ordered pair that is a solution of both equations.
The system has

_____.

C $\begin{cases} y = 3x - 3 \\ y = 3(x - 1) \end{cases}$

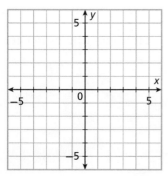

Start by graphing each function.

Identify if there are any ordered pairs that are solutions of both equations.

The graphs overlap, so every ordered pair that is a solution of one equation is also a solution of the other equation. The system has

_____.

Keisha and her friends visit the concession stand at a football game. The stand charges $2 for a hot dog and $1 for a drink. The friends buy a total of 8 items for $11. Tell how many hot dogs and how many drinks they bought.

A Let *x* represent the number of hot dogs they bought and *y* represent the number of drinks they bought.

Write an equation representing the **number of items they purchased**.

Number of hot dogs   +   Number of drinks   =   Total items

⬜   +   ⬜   =   ⬜

Write an equation representing the **money spent on the items**.

Cost of 1 hot dog times   +   Cost of 1 drink times   =   Total cost
number of hot dogs   number of drinks

⬜   +   ⬜   =   ⬜

B Write your equations in slope-intercept form.

_____

C Graph the solutions of both equations.

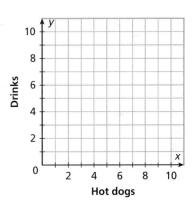

D Use the graph to identify the solution of the system of equations. Check your answer by substituting the ordered pair into both equations.

The point _____ is a solution of both equations.

E Interpret the solution in the original context.

Keisha and her friends bought _____ hot dog(s) and _____ drink(s).

REFLECT

3. **Conjecture** Why do you think the graph is limited to the first quadrant?

_____

_____

Solve each system by graphing.

1. $\begin{cases} 2x - 4y = 10 \\ x + y = 2 \end{cases}$ _____

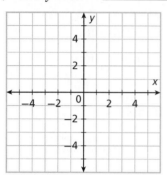

2. $\begin{cases} 2x - y = 0 \\ x + y = -6 \end{cases}$ _____

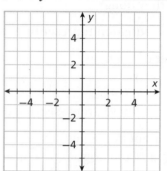

Graph each system and tell how many solutions the system has.

3. $\begin{cases} x - 3y = 2 \\ -3x + 9y = -6 \end{cases}$

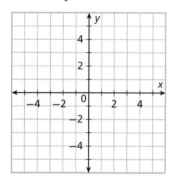

4. $\begin{cases} 2x - y = 5 \\ 2x - y = -1 \end{cases}$

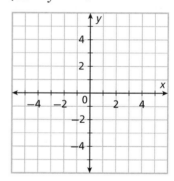

_____ solutions   _____ solutions

Mrs. Morales wrote a test with 15 questions covering spelling and vocabulary. Spelling questions (x) are worth 5 points and vocabulary questions (y) are worth 10 points. The maximum number of points possible on the test is 100.

5. Write an equation in slope-intercept form to represent the number of questions on the test.

_____

6. Write an equation in slope-intercept form to represent the total points on the test.

_____

7. Graph the solutions of both equations.

8. Use your graph to tell how many of each question type are on the test.

_____ spelling questions; _____ vocabulary questions

Solving Systems Algebraically

COMMON CORE

CC.8.EE.8b
CC.8.EE.8c

Essential question: *How can you solve a system of equations algebraically?*

You have already seen how to solve a system of equations by graphing. Now you will learn to solve systems using algebra.

1 EXAMPLE **Solving Systems Algebraically**

Solve each system algebraically.

A $\begin{cases} y = 7x + 10 \\ y = 9x + 38 \end{cases}$

$7x + 10 = 9x + 38$

Substitute the expression for y given in the first equation for the value of y in the second equation.

$\underline{}\underline{}$

$ = + 38$

$\underline{}\underline{}$

$ = $

$ = x$

Then use properties of equality to solve the equation for x.

Substitute the value of x into one of the original equations to solve for y.

The solution of the system is (_____, _____).

B $\begin{cases} 3x + 4y = 31 \\ 2x - y = 6 \end{cases}$

$2x - y = 6$

$\underline{}\underline{}$

$-y = 6 - $

$-y(-1) = \left(6 - \right)(-1)$

$ = -6 + $

Solve one equation for one of the variables. Because y is by itself in the second equation, solving that equation for y is a good place to start.

$3x + 4y = 31$

$3x + 4\left(\right) = 31$

$3x + (-24) + = 31$

$11x - 24 = 31$

$\underline{}\underline{}$

$11x = $

$x = $

Substitute the expression for y into the first equation and solve for x.

Substitute the value of x into one of the
original equations to solve for y.

The solution of the system is (_____, _____).

REFLECT

1. How can you check your answer?

_____

_____

You can use a graph to estimate the solution of a system of equations before solving algebraically.

2 EXAMPLE Using a Graph to Estimate the Solution of a System

Solve the system $\begin{cases} x - 4y = 4 \\ 2x - 3y = -3 \end{cases}$.

A Sketch a graph of each linear function by substituting some values for x and generating values of y.

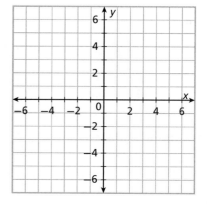

B The lines appear to intersect near $(-5, -2)$. How can you tell whether $(-5, -2)$ is the solution of the system?

_____

_____

_____

_____

_____

C Solve the system algebraically.

The solution is (_____, _____).

D Use the estimate you made using the graph to judge the reasonableness of your solution.

_____

_____

REFLECT

2. How can you determine that the system $\begin{cases} 5x - 2y = 8 \\ 5x - 2y = -3 \end{cases}$ has no solution without graphing or using algebraic methods?

_____

3 E X A M P L E   **Problem Solving with Systems of Equations**

Aaargh! There's pirate treasure to be found,
So search on the island, all around.
Draw a line through A and B.
Then a second line through C and D.
Dance a jig, "X" marks the spot,
If the lines intersect, that's the treasure's plot!

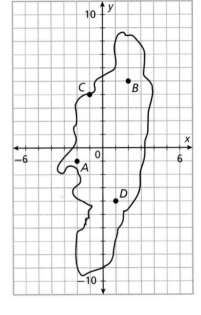

A Give the coordinates of each point and find the slope of the line through each pair of points.

A: (_____, _____)   C: (_____, _____)

B: (_____, _____)   D: (_____, _____)

Slope: Slope:

B Use the slopes of the lines to determine whether they will intersect.

_____

_____

C Write equations in slope-intercept form describing the line through points A and B and the line through points C and D.

Line through A and B: Line through C and D:

D Solve the system algebraically.

The solution is (_____, _____).

PRACTICE

Solve each system of equations algebraically.

1. $\begin{cases} y = \frac{2}{3}x - 5 \\ y = -x + 10 \end{cases}$

2. $\begin{cases} 3x + 2y = 9 \\ y = 4x - 1 \end{cases}$

3. $\begin{cases} 5x - 2y = 4 \\ 2x - y = 1 \end{cases}$

_____ _____ _____

4. **Error Analysis** Zach solves the system $\begin{cases} x + y = -3 \\ x - y = 1 \end{cases}$ and finds the solution $(1, -2)$.

Use a graph to explain whether Zach's solution is reasonable.

_____

_____

_____

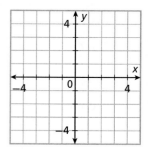

5. **Error Analysis** Angelica solves the system $\begin{cases} 3x - y = 0 \\ \frac{1}{4}x + \frac{3}{4}y = \frac{5}{2} \end{cases}$

and finds the solution $(1, 3)$. Use substitution to explain whether Angelica's solution is correct.

_____

_____

Angelo bought apples and bananas at the fruit stand. He bought 20 pieces of fruit and spent $11.50. Apples cost $0.50 and bananas cost $0.75 each.

6. Write a system of equations to model the problem. (Hint: One equation will represent the number of pieces of fruit. A second equation will represent the money spent on the fruit.)

_____

7. Solve the system algebraically. Tell how many apples and bananas Angelo bought.

_____

Problem Solving Connections

Is the Price Right? Travelers who arrive at an aiport usually have transportation options for getting to their next destination. Most travelers can choose between taxi or shuttle services to get to their hotels.

COMMON
CORE

CC.8.EE.7a,
CC.8.EE.7b,
CC.8.EE.8a,
CC.8.EE.8b,
CC.8.EE.8c

1 Writing Equations

Jackie just arrived at the Orlando International Airport. There are two routes from the airport to Jackie's hotel:

- If the driver uses city streets, the distance to the hotel is 29 miles.

- If the driver takes the expressway, the distance is only 23 miles, but Jackie will pay an additional $2.75 in toll charges.

A The first taxi company Jackie talks to charges an initial fee of $2.00 plus $2.40 for each mile. Write an equation to show the total charge y for traveling x miles.

_____

B Calculate the total cost to travel to Jackie's hotel taking each route.

Streets: Expressway:

Which route should Jackie instruct the driver to take? Why?

_____

C Jackie learns that the taxi can transport up to 4 people to the same destination at the rates given above. There is a $3 charge for each additional person. A shuttle bus company offers transportation to the hotel for $15 per person. Jackie is traveling with 3 friends. Calculate the total cost for Jackie and her friends to take the taxi along the expressway and the shuttle.

Taxi: Shuttle:

Should Jackie and her friends choose the taxi or the shuttle? Explain.

_____

2 Graphing a System

Chuck and his family are also vacationing in Florida. He researches taxi rates before they leave home. There are 5 people in Chuck's family (including Chuck).

Company 1: $2 initial fee, plus $2.40 per mile for 1 to 2 passengers and $3 per person for each additional person.

Company 2: $3.75 initial fee, plus $2.00 per mile for 1 to 2 passengers and $1.50 per person for each additional person.

Company 3: $3.85 initial fee, plus $2.20 per mile for up to 5 passengers.

A Write equations in slope-intercept form to model each company's fare y for traveling x miles with 5 passengers.

> Company 1:   Company 2:   Company 3:

B Sketch a graph of the system.

C Explain any restrictions that should be placed on the values of x and y.

_____

_____

_____

_____

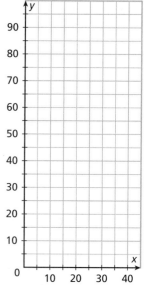

D The distance from the airport to the hotel where Chuck and his family are staying is 35 miles. Use your graph to determine which company is most expensive for Chuck's family of five to get to their hotel. Which company is least expensive?

_____

_____

E How could you check your answers to **D** ?

_____

_____

3 Solving a System of Equations Algebraically

Chuck's family decides to change their hotel reservation. They also learn that taxi company 1 will not be in operation on they day they need transportation.

A Chuck has not yet determined the distance between the airport and his family's new hotel. Explain how to use the graph from **2** to help Chuck's family choose the best value.

_____

_____

_____

_____

B Can you use the graph to determine which company is less expensive for a distance of 23 miles? If not, what method can you use?

_____

_____

_____

C Use algebraic methods to solve the system of equations representing fares for company 2 and company 3.

D Explain what your solution means in the context of the problem.

_____

_____

_____

_____

E Which company should Chuck's family choose to travel 23 miles to their new hotel?

_____

4 Looking Back at the Context

A What factors do you need to consider when analyzing transportation costs?

_____

_____

_____

B Suppose two companies have the same rate per mile but different initial fees. Describe what the graph representing their fares would look like. What is the solution of the system of equations representing the fares? Which company has the lower fare?

_____

_____

_____

_____

_____

C Suppose two companies have the same initial fees but different rates per mile. Describe what the graph representing their fares would look like. What is the solution of the system of equations representing the fares? Which company has the lower fare?

_____

_____

_____

_____

_____

D Why is it important to put restrictions on the values of x and y in a real-world problem?

_____

_____

_____

_____

_____

Name _____ Class _____ Date _____

MULTIPLE CHOICE

1. Which value of x makes the equation $5(x - 2) - 4 = 6$ true?

A. 2   **C.** 4

B. 3   **D.** 5

2. Which has the same solution as $2(x + 4) = -7 - 3x$?

F. $5x = 15$

G. $-5x = 15$

H. $-x = 11$

J. $x = 15$

3. How many solutions does the equation $2(x - 5) = 2x + 3$ have?

A. 0   **C.** 2

B. 1   **D.** infinitely many

4. How many solutions does the equation $4x + 28 = 4(x + 3) + 16$ have?

F. 0   **H.** 2

G. 1   **J.** infinitely many

5. Which ordered pair is the solution to the system of equations?

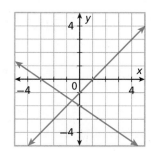

A. $\left(\frac{3}{5}, \frac{8}{5}\right)$ **C.** $\left(-\frac{3}{5}, \frac{8}{5}\right)$

B. $\left(\frac{3}{5}, -\frac{8}{5}\right)$ **D.** $\left(-\frac{3}{5}, -\frac{8}{5}\right)$

6. Which equation can you use to solve the system of equations shown?

$$\begin{cases} -4x + y = 3 \\ 11x - 5y = 16 \end{cases}$$

F. $11(4x + 3) - 5y = 16$

G. $11x - 5(4x + 3) = 16$

H. $-4(11x - 5y) = 3$

J. $-4x + 16 - 11x = 3$

7. Students from Thornebrooke Elementary are going on a field trip to an amusement park. Those who have annual passes will pay $10. Other students will pay $35. The school collected $1,375 for 50 students.

Which system of linear equations models this situation?

A. $\begin{cases} 10x + 35y = 50 \\ x + y = 1{,}375 \end{cases}$

B. $\begin{cases} 10x + 35y = 1{,}375 \\ x + y = 50 \end{cases}$

C. $\begin{cases} 10x + y = 50 \\ 35x + y = 1{,}375 \end{cases}$

D. $\begin{cases} 10x + y = 1{,}375 \\ x + 35y = 50 \end{cases}$

8. Which ordered pair is a solution of the system shown?

$$\begin{cases} -4x + 5y = 14 \\ 7x + 3y = -1 \end{cases}$$

F. $(1, 2)$

G. $(1, -2)$

H. $(-1, 2)$

J. $(-1, -2)$

9. Which graph represents a system of equations with no solution?

A.

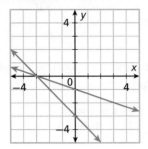

B.

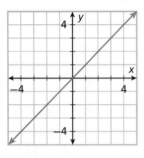

C.

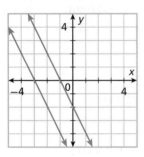

D.

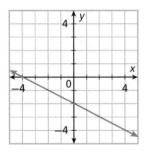

FREE RESPONSE

10. Dani solves the system of equations shown and finds that the solution is $(-2, 7)$. Explain whether Dani is correct.

$$\begin{cases} 7x - y = 7 \\ -3x + 2y = 8 \end{cases}$$

11. Graph the linear functions. Describe the solution set for the system of equations.

$$\begin{cases} 3x - y = 4 \\ -6x + 2y = 2 \end{cases}$$

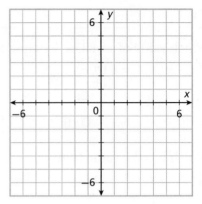

12. Solve the system by graphing.

$$\begin{cases} y = -2x + 5 \\ y = 2x + 1 \end{cases}$$

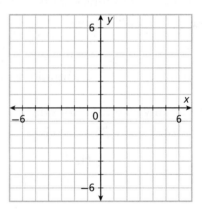

13. Solve the equation $5(x - 2) + 3 = 7x - 9$.

Geometry: Transformations

Unit Focus

In this unit, you will explore mathematical functions that move objects in specified ways in the coordinate plane. A translation slides a figure up or down and left or right without changing its size or shape. A reflection flips a figure of a line to create a mirror image. A rotation turns a figure to have a different orientation. A dilation expands or reduces a figure to have a different size but the same shape.

Unit at a Glance

COMMON CORE

Unpacking the Common Core State Standards

Use the table to help you understand the Common Core State Standards that are taught in this unit. Refer to the lessons listed after each standard for exploration and practice.

COMMON CORE Standards for Mathematical Content	What It Means For You
CC.8.G.1 Verify experimentally the properties of rotations, reflections, and translations: **a.** Lines are taken to lines, and line segments to line segments of the same length. **b.** Angles are taken to angles of the same measure. **c.** Parallel lines are taken to parallel lines. Lesson 4-2	Translations, reflections, and rotations are called rigid transformations because they do not change the size or shape of a figure. Characteristics such as the length of line segments, angle measures, and parallel lines are unchanged by these three types of transformations.
CC.8.G.2 Understand that a two-dimensional figure is congruent to another if the second can be obtained from the first by a sequence of rotations, reflections, and translations; given two congruent figures, describe a sequence that exhibits the congruence between them. Lesson 4-3	Because size and shape are preserved under translations, reflections, and rotations, the result of these transformations is an exact copy of the original figure. When two figures have the exact same size and shape, they are called congruent figures.
CC.8.G.3 Describe the effect of dilations, translations, rotations, and reflections on two-dimensional figures using coordinates. Lessons 4-1, 4-4	When you apply transformations to figures in the coordinate plane, you can describe the results of the transformation by giving the coordinates of the vertices of the figures. For some of these transformations, it is easy to write a general rule that describes what happens to each coordinate under the transformation.
CC.8.G.4 Understand that a two-dimensional figure is similar to another if the second can be obtained from the first by a sequence of rotations, reflections, translations, and dilations; given two similar two-dimensional figures, describe a sequence that exhibits the similarity between them. Lesson 4-5	A dilation changes the size of a figure but not its shape. When two figures have the same shape but different sizes, they are called similar figures.

Translations, Reflections, and Rotations

COMMON CORE

CC.8.G.3

Essential question: *How can you use coordinates to describe the result of a translation, reflection, or rotation?*

You learned that a function is a rule that assigns exactly one output to each input. A **transformation** is a type of function that describes a change in the position, size, or shape of a figure. The input of a transformation is called the **preimage**, and the output of a transformation is called the **image**.

A **translation** is a transformation that slides a figure along a straight line. The image has the same size and shape as the preimage.

1 EXPLORE   **Applying Translations**

The triangle is the preimage (input). The arrow shows the motion of a translation and how point A is translated to point A'.

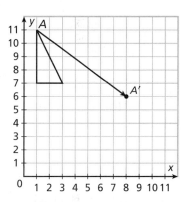

A Trace the triangle on a piece of paper. Slide point A of your traced triangle down the arrow to model the translation.

B Sketch the image (output) of the translation.

C Describe the motion modeled by the translation.

Move _____ units right and _____ units down.

D Complete the ordered pairs to describe the effect of the translation on point A.

$(1, 11)$ becomes $\left(1 + \boxed{}, 11 + \boxed{}\right) = \left(\boxed{}, \boxed{}\right)$

E You can give a general rule for a translation by telling the number of units to move up or down and the number of units to move left or right. Complete the ordered pairs to write a general rule for this transformation.

$(x, y) \rightarrow \left(x + \boxed{}, y + \boxed{}\right)$

TRY THIS!

1. Apply the translation $(x, y) \rightarrow (x - 2, y + 3)$ to the figure shown. Give the coordinates of the vertices of the image. (The image of point A is point A'.)

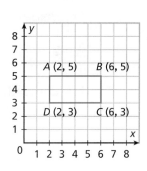

A': (_____, _____)

B': (_____, _____)

C': (_____, _____)

D': (_____, _____)

A **reflection** is a transformation that flips a figure across a line called the **line of reflection**. Each point and its image are the same distance from the line of reflection. The image has the same size and shape as the preimage.

The triangle is the preimage. You will use the *x*- or *y*-axis as the line of reflection.

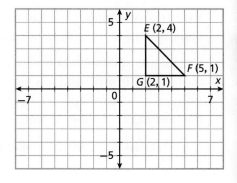

Reflection across the *x*-axis:

A Trace the triangle and the *x*- and *y*-axes on a piece of paper. Fold your paper along the *x*-axis and trace the image of the triangle on the opposite side of the *x*-axis.

B Sketch the image of the reflection. Label each vertex of the image. (The image of point *E* is point *E'*.)

C Complete the table.

Preimage	(2, 4)	(2, 1)	(5, 1)
Image			

D How does reflecting the figure across the *x*-axis change the *x*-coordinates? How does it change the *y*-coordinates?

_____

E Complete the ordered pair to write a general rule for reflection across the *x*-axis. $(x, y) \rightarrow \left(x, y \times \boxed{} \right)$

Reflection across the *y*-axis:

F Fold your traced image along the *y*-axis and trace the image of the triangle on the opposite side of the *y*-axis.

G Sketch the image of the reflection. Label each vertex of the image. (For clarity, label the image of point *E* as point *E''*.)

H Complete the table.

Preimage	(2, 4)	(2, 1)	(5, 1)
Image			

I How does reflecting the figure across the *y*-axis change the *x*-coordinates? How does it change the *y*-coordinates?

_____

J Complete the ordered pair to write a general rule for reflection across the *y*-axis. $(x, y) \rightarrow \left(\boxed{}, \boxed{} \right)$

Rules for Reflections

Across the *x*-axis	$(x, y) \rightarrow (x, -y)$
Across the *y*-axis	$(x, y) \rightarrow (-x, y)$

A **rotation** is a transformation that turns a figure around a given point called the center of rotation. The image has the same size and shape as the preimage.

3 EXPLORE Applying Rotations

The triangle is the preimage. You will use the origin as the center of rotation.

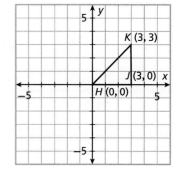

A Trace the triangle on a piece of paper. Rotate the triangle 90° counterclockwise about the origin. The side of the triangle that lies along the *x*-axis should now lie along the *y*-axis.

B Sketch the image of the rotation. Label each vertex of the image. (The image of point *H* is point *H'*.)

C Give the coordinates of the vertices of the image.

H': (_____, _____)

J': (_____, _____)

K': (_____, _____)

TRY THIS!

3a. Rotate the original triangle 180° counterclockwise about the origin. Sketch the result on the coordinate grid above. Label each vertex of the image. (For clarity, label the image of point *H* as point *H''*.)

3b. Give the coordinates of the vertices of the image.

H'': (_____, _____)

J'': (_____, _____)

K'': (_____, _____)

REFLECT

3c. Compare the image of a counterclockwise rotation of 180° about the origin to the image of a clockwise rotation of 180° about the origin.

_____

3d. Through how many degrees would you need to rotate a figure for the image to coincide with the preimage? Explain.

_____

_____

PRACTICE

Sketch the image of the figure after the given transformation.
Label each vertex.

1. Translation: $(x, y) \rightarrow (x - 3, y + 1)$

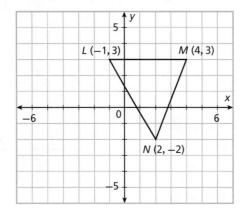

2. Reflection: $(x, y) \rightarrow (x, -y)$

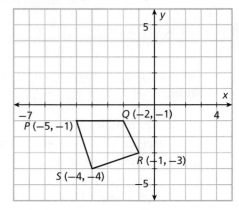

3. Rotation: 90° clockwise about the origin

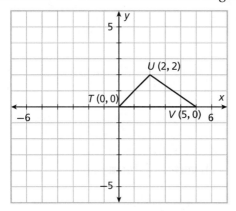

4. Reflection: $(x, y) \rightarrow (-x, y)$

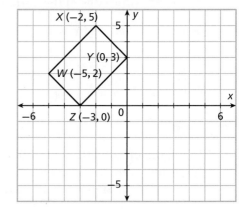

Apply each transformation to the vertices of the original rectangle,
and give the coordinates of each vertex of the image.

Vertices of Rectangle	(2, 2)	(2, 4)	(−3, 4)	(−3, 2)
5. $(x, y) \rightarrow (x, -y)$				
6. $(x, y) \rightarrow (x + 2, y - 5)$				
7. $(x, y) \rightarrow (-x, y)$				
8. $(x, y) \rightarrow (-x, -y)$				
9. $(x, y) \rightarrow (x - 3, y + 1)$				

4-2

Properties of Transformations

Essential question: *What properties of a figure are preserved under a translation, reflection, or rotation?*

COMMON CORE

CC.8.G.1

1 **E X P L O R E**   **Properties of Translations**

A   Trace the rectangle and triangle on a piece of paper. Then cut out your traced figures.

B   Place your copy of the rectangle on top of the rectangle in the figure. Then translate the rectangle by sliding your copy 6 units to the right and 1 unit down. Draw the new location of the rectangle on the coordinate plane and label the vertices A', B', C', and D'.

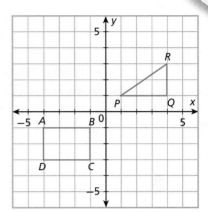

C   Place your copy of the triangle on top of the triangle in the figure. Then translate the triangle by sliding your copy 5 units to the left and 2 units up. Draw the new location of the triangle on the coordinate plane and label the vertices P', Q', and R'.

D   Use a ruler to measure line segments $\overline{AD}$ and $\overline{PR}$. Then, measure $\overline{A'D'}$ and $\overline{P'R'}$. What do you notice?

_____

E   Use a protractor to measure $\angle C$ and $\angle R$. Then, measure $\angle C'$ and $\angle R'$. What do you notice?

_____

F   Count the pairs of parallel lines in rectangle $ABCD$. Count the pairs of parallel lines in rectangle $A'B'C'D'$. What do you notice?

_____

_____

REFLECT

1a.   Use your results from **D**, **E**, and **F** to write a conjecture about translations.

_____

A Trace the rectangle and triangle on a piece of paper. Then, cut out your traced figures.

B Place your copy of the rectangle on top of the rectangle in the figure. Then reflect the rectangle across the *x*-axis by flipping your copy across the *x*-axis. Draw the new location of the rectangle on the coordinate plane and label the vertices *A'*, *B'*, *C'*, and *D'*.

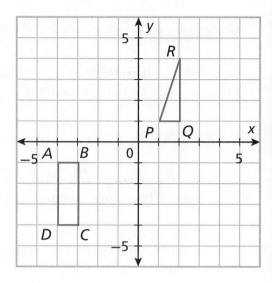

C Place your copy of the triangle on top of the triangle in the figure. Then reflect the triangle across the *y*-axis by flipping your copy across the *y*-axis. Draw the new location of the triangle on the coordinate plane and label the vertices *P'*, *Q'*, and *R'*.

D Use a ruler to measure line segments $\overline{BC}$ and $\overline{PR}$. Then, measure $\overline{B'C'}$ and $\overline{P'R'}$. What do you notice?

_____

E Use a protractor to measure ∠*D* and ∠*P*. Then, measure ∠*D'* and ∠*P'*. What do you notice?

_____

F Count the pairs of parallel lines in rectangle *ABCD*. Count the pairs of parallel lines in rectangle *A'B'C'D'*. What do you notice?

_____

REFLECT

2a. Use your results from **D** , **E** , and **F** to write a conjecture about reflections.

_____

TRY THIS!

2b. Rotate your copy of the triangle from **A** 180° around the origin and draw the new location of the triangle. Make measurements and observations to help you state a conjecture about rotations.

_____

_____

_____

Transformations and Congruence

COMMON
CORE

CC.8.G.2

Essential question: *What is the connection between transformations and figures that have the same shape and size?*

1 EXPLORE   Combining Transformations

Apply the indicated series of transformations to the triangle. Each transformation is applied to the image of the previous translation, not the original figure. Label each image with the letter of the transformation applied.

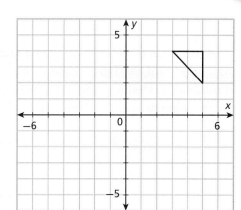

A   Reflection across the *x*-axis

B $(x, y) \rightarrow (x - 3, y)$

C   Reflection across the *y*-axis

D $(x, y) \rightarrow (x, y + 4)$

E   Rotation 90° clockwise around the origin

F   Compare the size and shape of the final image to that of the original figure.

_____

Two figures are said to be **congruent** if one can be obtained from the other by a sequence of translations, reflections, and rotations. Congruent figures have the same size and shape.

When you are told that two figures are congruent, there must be a sequence of translations, reflections, and/or rotations that transforms one into the other.

2 EXAMPLE   Congruent Figures

A   Identify a sequence of transformations that will transform figure *A* into figure *B*.

_____

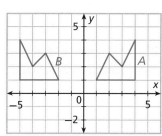

B   Identify another sequence of transformations that transforms figure *A* into figure *B*.

_____

C Any sequence of transformations that changes figure *B* into figure *C* will need to include a rotation. Identify a rotation around the origin that would result in the figure being oriented as figure *C*.

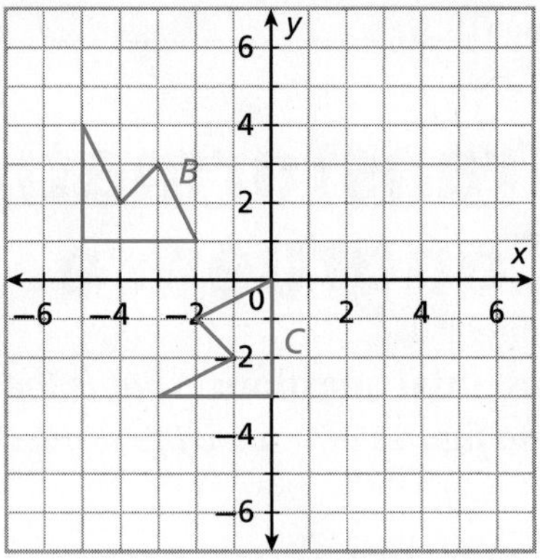

_____° clockwise / counterclockwise

D After the rotation you identified in **C**, what transformation is necessary to result in figure *C*?

_____

_____

E A sequence of transformations that changes figure *D* to figure *E* will need to include a rotation. Describe a rotation around the origin that would result in the figure being oriented as figure *E*.

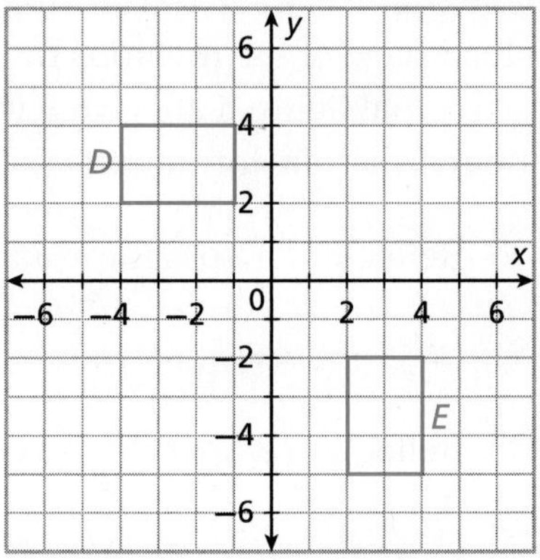

_____° clockwise / counterclockwise

F After the rotation you identified in **E**, what are the coordinates of the vertices of the rotated figure?

_____

G After the rotation you identified in **E**, what transformation is necessary to result in figure *E*?

_____

_____

TRY THIS!

1. Explain whether the figures are congruent.

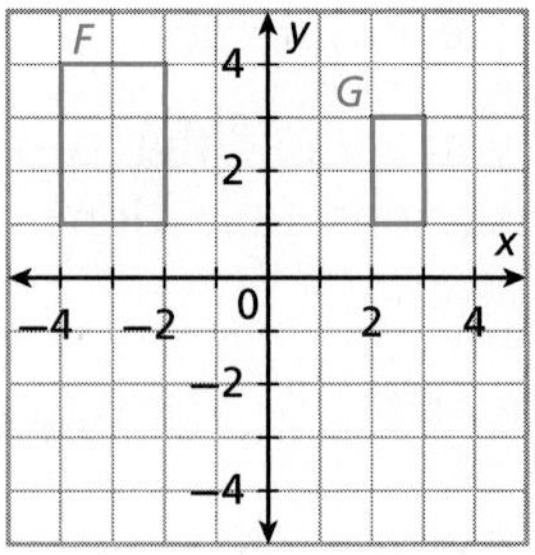

_____

_____

_____

_____

2. Describe a sequence of translations, reflections, or rotations that would transform figure *F* into figure *G*.

_____

_____

_____

Dilations

Essential question: *How can you use coordinates to describe the result of a dilation?*

COMMON CORE

CC.8.G.3

A **dilation** is a transformation that changes the size, but not the shape, of a geometric figure. The center of the figure is known as the **center of dilation**. When dilating in the coordinate plane, the center of dilation is usually the origin.

1 EXPLORE   **Applying Dilations**

The square is the preimage (input). The center of dilation is the origin.

A   List the coordinates of the vertices of the square.

A: (_____ , _____)   C: (_____ , _____)

B: (_____ , _____)   D: (_____ , _____)

B   Multiply each coordinate by 2. List the resulting ordered pairs.

A': (_____ , _____)   C': (_____ , _____)

B': (_____ , _____)   D': (_____ , _____)

C   Sketch the image of the dilation. Label each vertex of the image.

D   How does multiplying the coordinates of the preimage by 2 affect the image?

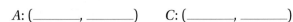

_____

_____

E   Multiply each coordinate from the preimage by $\frac{1}{2}$. List the resulting ordered pairs.

A'': (_____ , _____)   C'': (_____ , _____)

B'': (_____ , _____)   D'': (_____ , _____)

F   Sketch the image of the dilation. Label each vertex of the image.

G   How does multiplying the coordinates of the preimage by $\frac{1}{2}$ affect the image?

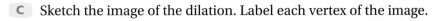

_____

_____

A **scale factor** describes how much larger or smaller the image of a dilation is than the preimage.

 Rule for Dilation

For a dilation centered at the origin with scale factor k, the image of point $P(x, y)$ is found by multiplying each coordinate by k.

$$(x, y) \rightarrow (kx, ky)$$

- If $k > 1$, then the image is larger than the preimage.
- If $0 < k < 1$, then the image is smaller than the preimage.

2 EXAMPLE Enlargements

The figure is the preimage. The center of dilation is the origin.

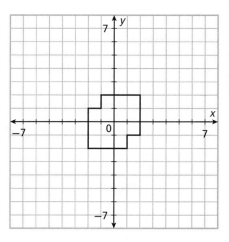

A List the coordinates of the vertices of the preimage in the first column of the table.

Preimage	Image
(2, 2)	(6, 6)

B What is the scale factor for the dilation $(x, y) \rightarrow (3x, 3y)$? _____

C Apply the dilation to the preimage and write the coordinates of the vertices of the image in the second column of the table.

D Sketch the image under the dilation on the coordinate grid.

REFLECT

2a. How does the dilation affect the length of line segments?

_____

_____

2b. How does the dilation affect angle measures?

_____

The arrow is the preimage. The center of dilation is the origin.

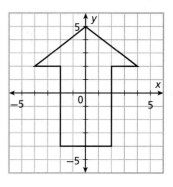

A List the coordinates of the vertices of the preimage in the first column of the table.

Preimage	Image

B What is the scale factor for the dilation $(x, y) \to \left(\frac{1}{2}x, \frac{1}{2}y\right)$? _____

C Apply the dilation to the preimage and write the coordinates of the vertices of the image in the second column of the table.

D Sketch the image under the dilation on the coordinate grid.

REFLECT

3a. How does the dilation affect the length of line segments?

_____

_____

3b. How would a dilation with scale factor 1 affect the preimage?

_____

_____

TRY THIS!

3c. Identify the scale factor of the dilation shown.

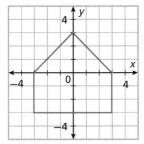  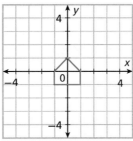

_____

1. The square is the preimage. The center of dilation is the origin. Write the coordinates of the vertices of the preimage in the first column of the table. Then apply the dilation $(x, y) \rightarrow \left(\frac{3}{2}x, \frac{3}{2}y\right)$ and write the coordinates of the vertices of the image in the second column. Sketch the image of the figure under the dilation.

Preimage	Image
(2, 0)	(3, 0)

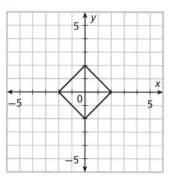

Sketch the image of the figure under the given dilation.

2. $(x, y) \rightarrow (2x, 2y)$

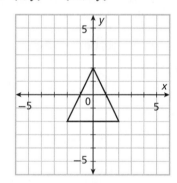

3. $(x, y) \rightarrow \left(\frac{2}{3}x, \frac{2}{3}y\right)$

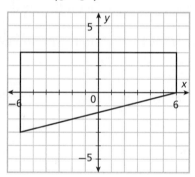

Identify the scale factor of the dilation shown.

4. scale factor =

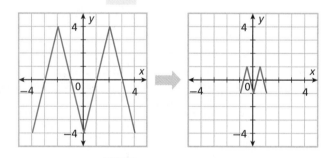

5. scale factor =

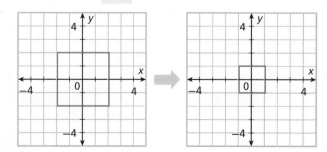

Transformations and Similarity

COMMON
CORE

CC.8.G.4

Essential question: *What is the connection between transformations and similar figures?*

1 **EXPLORE** **Combining Transformations with Dilations**

Apply the indicated series of transformations to the rectangle. Each transformation is applied to the image of the previous transformation, not to the original figure. Label each image with the letter of the transformation applied.

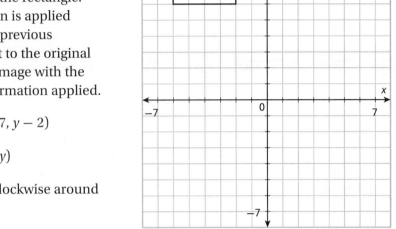

A $(x, y) \rightarrow (x + 7, y - 2)$

B $(x, y) \rightarrow (x, -y)$

C rotation 90° clockwise around the origin

D $(x, y) \rightarrow (x + 5, y + 3)$

E $(x, y) \rightarrow (3x, 3y)$

F List the coordinates of the vertices of rectangle E.

_____

G Compare the following attributes of rectangle E to those of the original figure.

Shape	
Size	
Angle Measures	

Two figures are **similar** if one can be obtained from the other by a sequence of translations, reflections, rotations, and dilations. Similar figures have the same shape but may be different sizes.

When you are told that two figures are similar, there must be a sequence of translations, reflections, rotations, and/or dilations that can transform one to the other.

2 EXPLORE   Similar Figures

A Identify a sequence of transformations that will transform figure *A* into figure *B*.

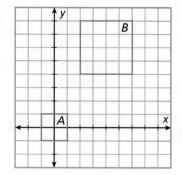

_____

_____

B What happens if you reverse the order of the sequence you defined in **A**?

_____

_____

C Tell whether figures *A* and *B* are congruent. Tell whether they are similar.

_____

_____

D Identify a sequence of transformations that will transform figure *C* into figure *D*. Include a reflection.

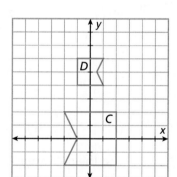

_____

_____

E Identify a sequence of transformations that will transform figure *C* into figure *D*. Include a rotation.

_____

_____

TRY THIS!

1. Circle the figures that are similar to each other.

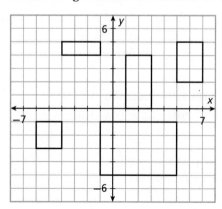

Problem Solving Connections

Stitch Perfect Ellie is making a cross-stitch pattern for a butterfly. She uses translations, reflection, rotations, and dilations to design the parts of the butterfly. Perform the transformations as described. Then, draw the images on the final answer grid on the last page of the Problem Solving Connections.

COMMON CORE

CC.8.G.1
CC.8.G.2
CC.8.G.3
CC.8.G.4

1 Making the Body and Wings

A The coordinates of the vertices of the rectangle that represents the body of the butterfly are $(-1, 7)$, $(1, 7)$, $(1, -7)$, $(-1, -7)$. Draw the body on the final answer grid.

B What would the body of the butterfly look like if it were rotated clockwise by 180°?

_____

_____

C Ellie draws one upper wing of the butterfly. The coordinates of the vertices of the wing are given in the table. Draw the wing on the final answer grid.

First Upper Wing	$(-10, 9)$	$(-4, 9)$	$(-1, 5)$	$(-1, 0)$	$(-10, 2)$
Image					

To find the coordinates of the other upper wing, perform a reflection across the y-axis. Draw the image of the first wing on the final answer grid.

D Ellie draws one lower wing of the butterfly. The coordinates of the vertices of the wing are given in the table. Draw the wing on the final answer grid.

First Lower Wing	$(1, 0)$	$(5, 0)$	$(9, -2)$	$(10, -9)$	$(5, -9)$	$(1, -2)$
Image						

To find the coordinates of the other lower wing, perform a reflection across the y-axis. Draw the image of the first wing on the final answer grid.

E Is the first upper wing congruent to its image? Is the first lower wing congruent to its image? Explain how you know.

_____

_____

2 Designing the Upper-Wing Pattern

A On the grid below, draw a square centered at the origin, with side lengths of 6 units.

B Ellie transforms the figure from **A** under the dilation $(x, y) \rightarrow \left(\frac{1}{3}x, \frac{1}{3}y\right)$. Write the coordinates of the image. Then, draw the image on the grid below.

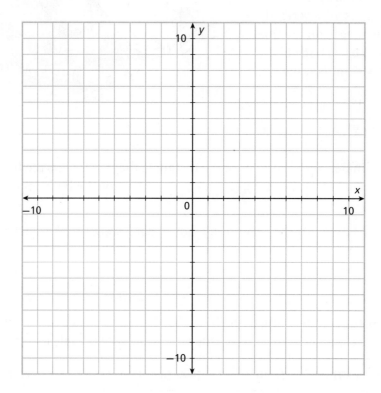

C Ellie transforms the figure from **B** under the translation $(x, y) \rightarrow (x + 5, y + 4)$. Write the coordinates of the image. Then, draw the image on the final answer grid.

D Ellie transforms the figure from **C** by reflecting it across the y-axis. Write the coordinates of the image. Then, draw the image on the final answer grid.

E On the final answer grid, there is a black square. Ellie reflects the square across the y-axis. Write the coordinates of the image. Then, draw the image on the final answer grid.

3 Designing the Lower-Wing Pattern

A On the final answer grid, there is a black triangle. Ellie reflects the triangle across the *y*-axis. Write the coordinates of the image. Then, draw the image on the final answer grid.

_____

B Ellie rotates the original triangle by 180° about the origin. Write the coordinates of the image. Then, draw the image on the grid below.

_____

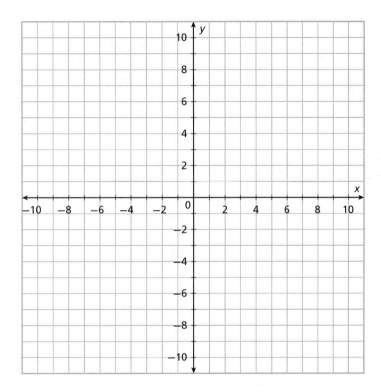

C Ellie transforms the figure from **B** under the translation $(x, y) \rightarrow (x - 13, y - 11)$. Write the coordinates of the image. Then, draw the image on the final answer grid.

_____

D Ellie transforms the figure from **C** by reflecting it across the *y*-axis. Write the coordinates of the image. Then, draw the image on the final answer grid.

_____

4 Final Answer Grid

Use this final answer grid to draw Ellie's completed butterfly design.

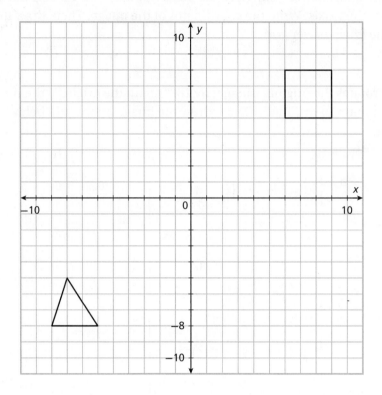

Are there any similar figures (that are not congruent) in Ellie's butterfly design? Use what you know about transformations and similarity to justify your answer. (If there are similar figures in the design, describe a sequence of transformations that would transform one of the similar figures to the other.)

_____

_____

_____

_____

_____

_____

_____

_____

Name _____ Class _____ Date _____

MULTIPLE CHOICE

1. Which is the image of $(2, 3)$ under the translation $(x, y) \rightarrow (x - 5, y - 2)$?

A. $(-5, -2)$ C. $(3, 5)$

B. $(-3, 1)$ D. $(3, -1)$

2. Which is the image of $(2, 3)$ under a reflection across the y-axis?

F. $(2, 3)$ H. $(2, -3)$

G. $(-2, 3)$ J. $(-2, -3)$

3. Which is the image of $(2, 3)$ under a 180° rotation about the origin?

A. $(3, 2)$ C. $(-2, -3)$

B. $(2, -3)$ D. $(-3, -2)$

4. Which sequence of translations, reflections, rotations, and/or dilations transforms figure A into figure B?

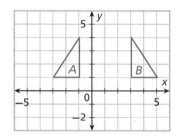

F. 180° rotation; reflection across y-axis

G. dilation with center at origin with scale factor of 2; translation 6 units left

H. reflection across the y-axis; translation 2 units right

J. reflection across the x-axis, dilation with center as origin with scale factor of $\frac{1}{2}$

Use the figure to answer 5 and 6.

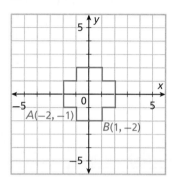

5. Which is the image of point A under a dilation centered at the origin described by the rule $(x, y) \rightarrow (4x, 4y)$?

A. $(8, 4)$ C. $\left(-\frac{1}{2}, -\frac{1}{4}\right)$

B. $\left(\frac{1}{2}, \frac{1}{4}\right)$ D. $(-8, -4)$

6. Which is the image of point B under a dilation centered at the origin with scale factor $\frac{1}{3}$?

F. $\left(\frac{1}{3}, -\frac{2}{3}\right)$ H. $\left(\frac{4}{3}, -\frac{5}{3}\right)$

G. $(3, -6)$ J. $(-3, 6)$

7. Which is not an image of the figure under a translation, reflection, rotation, or dilation?

A.   C.

B.   D.

8. Which is the scale factor for the dilation that transforms figure *C* into figure *D*?

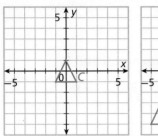 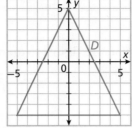

   F. $\frac{1}{5}$ **H.** 2

   G. $\frac{1}{2}$ **J.** 5

FREE RESPONSE

9. Draw a pair of figures that are similar but not congruent.

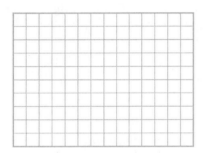

10. Give a sequence of translations, reflections, or rotations that will transform to figure *F* into figure *G*.

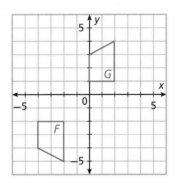

_____

_____

_____

11. Draw the image of the rectangle after a dilation with center at the origin and scale factor of 2, followed by a translation 2 units down.

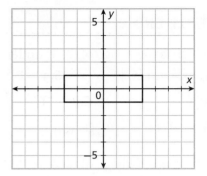

Use the figure for 12 through 15.

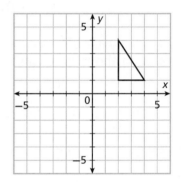

12. Sketch the image of the black figure under a reflection across the *x*-axis.

13. Sketch the image of the black figure after a rotation 90° counterclockwise about the origin followed by a translation left 1 unit.

14. Sketch the image of the black figure after a reflection across the *y*-axis followed by a reflection across the *x*-axis.

15. Identify another transformation or sequence of transformations that results in the same image as the result of Problem 14.

_____

_____

Geometry: Two- and Three-Dimensional Figures

Unit Focus

In this unit, you will use facts about lines and triangles to determine the sizes of unknown angles. You will establish rules for determining if two triangles are similar, and explain a proof of the Pythagorean Theorem. You will also learn the formulas for volume of cylinders, cones, and spheres.

Unit at a Glance

COMMON CORE

Lesson		Standards for Mathematical Content
5-1	Parallel Lines Cut by a Transversal	CC.8.G.5
5-2	Triangle Angle Theorems	CC.8.G.5
5-3	Similar Triangles	CC.8.G.5
5-4	Similar Triangles and Slope	CC.8.EE.6
5-5	Using the Pythagorean Theorem	CC.8.G.7, CC.8.G.8
5-6	Proving the Pythagorean Theorem	CC.8.G.6
5-7	Volume Formulas	CC.8.G.9
	Problem Solving Connections	
	Test Prep	

Unpacking the Common Core State Standards

Use the table to help you understand the Common Core State Standards that are taught in this unit. Refer to the lessons listed after each standard for exploration and practice.

COMMON CORE Standards for Mathematical Content	What It Means For You
CC.8.EE.6 Use similar triangles to explain why the slope *m* is the same between any two distinct points on a non-vertical line in the coordinate plane. Lesson 5-4	Given similar triangles, you will explain why the slope is the same between any two points.
CC.8.G.5 Use informal arguments to establish facts about the angle sum and exterior angle of triangles, about the angles created when parallel lines are cut by a transversal, and the angle-angle criterion for similarity of triangles. Lessons 5-1, 5-2, 5-3	You will learn about the special angle relationships formed when parallel lines are intersected by a third line called a transversal. You will learn that the sum of the angle measures in a triangle is the same for all triangles. You will learn one way to determine whether two triangles are similar.
CC.8.G.6 Explain a proof of the Pythagorean Theorem and its converse. Lesson 5-6	You will use an area model to prove the Pythagorean Theorem. You will also explore whether the converse (opposite) of the Pythagorean Theorem is true.
CC.8.G.7 Apply the Pythagorean Theorem to determine unknown side lengths in right triangles in real-world and mathematical problems in two and three dimensions. Lesson 5-5	You will use the Pythagorean Theorem to find the lengths of sides in a right triangle.
CC.8.G.8 Apply the Pythagorean Theorem to find the distance between two points in a coordinate system. Lesson 5-5	You will use the Pythagorean Theorem to find the hypotenuse of a right triangle in the coordinate plane.
CC.8.G.9 Know the formulas for the volumes of cones, cylinders, and spheres, and use them to solve real-world and mathematical problems. Lesson 5-7	You will learn the formulas for volume of a cylinder, cone, and sphere.

UNIT 5

Parallel Lines Cut by a Transversal

COMMON
CORE

CC.8.G.5

Essential question: *What can you conclude about the angles formed by parallel lines that are cut by a transversal?*

A **transversal** is a line that intersects two lines in the same plane at two different points. Transversal *t* and lines *a* and *b* form eight angles.

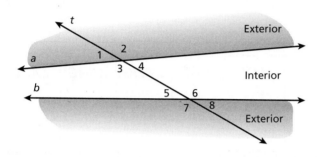

Angle Pairs Formed by a Transversal

Term	Example
Corresponding angles lie on the same side of the transversal *t*, on the same side of lines *a* and *b*.	∠1 and ∠5
Alternate interior angles are nonadjacent angles that lie on opposite sides of the transversal *t*, between lines *a* and *b*.	∠3 and ∠6
Alternate exterior angles lie on opposite sides of the transversal *t*, outside lines *a* and *b*.	∠1 and ∠8
Same-side interior angles lie on the same side of the transversal *t*, between lines *a* and *b*.	∠3 and ∠5

1 EXPLORE Parallel Lines and Transversals

Use geometry software to explore the angles formed when a transversal intersects parallel lines.

A Construct a line and label two points on the line *A* and *B*.

B Create point *C* not on $\overleftrightarrow{AB}$. Then construct a line parallel to $\overleftrightarrow{AB}$ through point *C*. Create another point on this line and label it *D*.

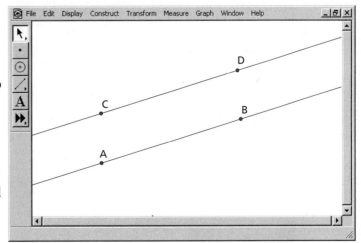

C Create two points outside the two parallel lines and label them *E* and *F*. Construct transversal $\overleftrightarrow{EF}$. Label the points of intersection *G* and *H*.

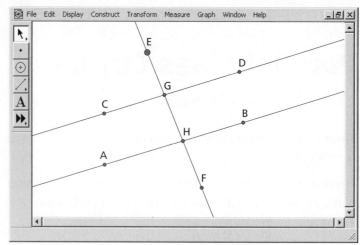

D Measure the angles formed by the parallel lines and the transversal. Write the angle measures in the table below.

E Drag point *E* or point *F* to a different position record the new angle measures in the table.

Angle	∠CGE	∠DGE	∠CGH	∠DGH	∠AHG	∠BHG	∠AHF	∠BHF
Measure								
Measure								

REFLECT

1a. Identify the pairs of corresponding angles in the diagram. Then make a conjecture about their angle measures. Drag a point in the diagram to confirm your conjecture.

_____

_____

1b. Identify the pairs of alternate interior angles in the diagram. Then make a conjecture about their angle measures. Drag a point in the diagram to confirm your conjecture.

_____

1c. Identify the pairs of alternate exterior angles in the diagram. Then make a conjecture about their angle measures. Drag a point in the diagram to confirm your conjecture.

_____

1d. Identify the pairs of same-side interior angles in the diagram. Then make a conjecture about their angle measures. Drag a point in the diagram to confirm your conjecture.

_____

_____

You can use your knowledge of transformations to informally justify the angle relationships formed by parallel lines and a transversal.

EXPLORE   Justifying Angle Relationships

Lines *a* and *b* are parallel. (The blue arrows on the diagram indicate parallel lines.)

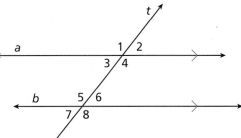

A   Trace line *a* and line *t* on a piece of paper. Label ∠1. Translate your traced angle down so that line *a* aligns with line *b* and line *t* aligns with itself. Which angle does ∠1 align with? _____

B   Because there is a translation that transforms ∠1 to _____, ∠1 and _____ are congruent.

TRY THIS!

2.   Name a pair of alternate interior angles. What transformation(s) could you use to show that that those angles are congruent?

_____

_____

EXAMPLE   Finding Unknown Angle Measures

Find each angle measure.

A   m∠5 when m∠4 = 55°

∠4 is congruent to ∠5 because they are

_____

m∠5 = _____°

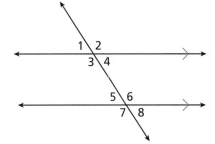

B   m∠*SVW*

∠*SVW* is _____ to ∠*YVW* because they are a linear pair.

∠*SVW* + ∠*YVW* = 180°

4*x*° + ☐° = 180°

☐*x* = 180°

$\dfrac{\boxed{}\,x}{\boxed{}} = \dfrac{180}{12}$

x = ☐

∠*SVW* = ∠8*x*° = $\left(8 \cdot \boxed{}\right)$° = ☐°

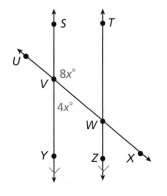

Use the figure for 1–4.

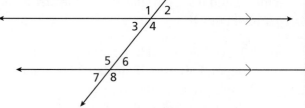

1. Name a pair of corresponding angles.

_____

2. Name a pair of alternate exterior angles.

_____

3. Name the relationship between ∠3 and ∠6.

_____

4. Name the relationship between ∠4 and ∠6.

_____

For parallel lines intersected by a transversal, tell whether each type of angle pair is congruent or supplementary.

5. alternate interior angles

_____

6. linear pair

_____

7. corresponding angles

_____

8. same-side interior angles

_____

9. vertical angles

_____

10. alternate exterior angles

_____

Find each angle measure.

11. m∠2 when m∠1 = 30°

_____

12. m∠6 when m∠1 = 30°

_____

13. m∠7 when m∠3 = 150°

_____

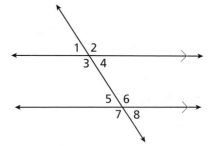

14. m∠EGB

_____

15. m∠AGH

_____

16. m∠DHF

_____

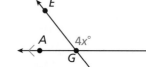

Triangle Angle Theorems

Essential question: *What can you conclude about the measures of the angles of a triangle?*

COMMON
CORE

CC.8.G.5

1 EXPLORE   Sum of the Angle Measures in a Triangle

There is a special relationship between the measures of the interior angles of a triangle.

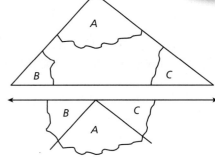

A   Draw a triangle and cut it out. Label the angles *A*, *B*, and *C*.

B   Tear off each "corner" of the triangle. Each corner includes the vertex of one angle of the triangle.

C   Arrange the vertices of the angle around a point so that none of your corners overlap and there are no gaps between them.

D   What do you notice about how the angles fit together around a point?

_____

E   What is the measure of a straight angle? _____

F   Describe the relationship among the measures of the angles of △*ABC* in words.

_____

The Triangle Sum Theorem states that for △*ABC*,
m∠*A* + m∠*B* + m∠*C* = _____.

TRY THIS!

Find the missing angle measure.

1a.

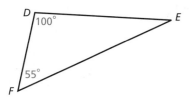

$$55° + \boxed{} + m\angle E = 180°$$
$$155° + m\angle E = 180°$$
$$155° - \boxed{} + m\angle E = 180° - \boxed{}$$
$$m\angle E = \boxed{}$$

1b.

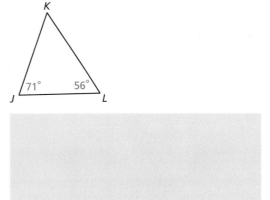

You can use your knowledge of parallel lines intersected by a transversal to informally justify the Triangle Sum Theorem.

2 EXPLORE   Justifying the Triangle Sum Theorem

Follow the steps to informally prove the Triangle Sum Theorem. You should draw each step on your own paper. The figures below are provided for you to check your work.

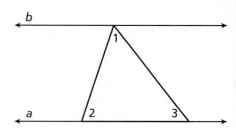

A Draw a triangle and label the angles as ∠1, ∠2, and ∠3 as shown.

B Draw line *a* through the base of the triangle.

C The Parallel Postulate states that through a point not on a line ℓ, there is exactly one line parallel to line ℓ. Draw line *b* parallel to line *a*, through the vertex opposite the base of the triangle.

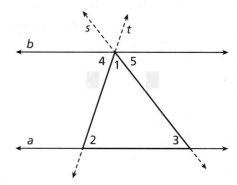

D Extend the other sides of the triangles to form transversal *s* and transversal *t*. Transversals *s* and *t* intersect parallel lines *a* and *b*.

E Label the angles formed by line *b* and the transversals as ∠4 and ∠5.

F ∠4 and _____ are alternate interior angles, so they are _____.
Label ∠4 with the number of the angle it is congruent to.

G ∠5 and _____ are alternate interior angles, so they are _____. Label ∠5 with the number of the angle it is congruent to.

H The three angles that lie along line *b* at the vertex of the triangle are ∠1 and two angles that have the same measures as ∠2 and ∠3. Because these three angles lie along a line, the sum of their measures is _____.

m∠1 + m∠2 + m∠3 = _____

The sum of the angle measures in a triangle is always _____.

An **interior angle** of a triangle is formed by two sides of the triangle. An **exterior angle** of a triangle is formed by one side of the triangle and the extension of an adjacent side. Each exterior angle has two *remote interior angles*. A **remote interior angle** is an interior angle that is not adjacent to the exterior angle.

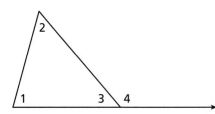

- ∠1, ∠2, and ∠3 are interior angles.
- ∠4 is an exterior angle.
- ∠1 and ∠2 are remote interior angles to ∠4.

3 **EXPLORE**   **Exterior Angles and Remote Interior Angles**

There is a special relationship between the measure of an exterior angle and the measures of its remote interior angles.

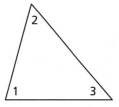

A Extend the base of the triangle and label the exterior angle as ∠4.

B The Triangle Sum Theorem states:

m∠1 + m∠2 + m∠3 = _____

C ∠3 and ∠4 form a _____,

so m∠3 + m∠4 = _____.

D Use the equations in **B** and **C** to complete the following equation:

m∠1 + m∠2 + _____ = _____ + m∠4

E Use properties of equality to simplify the equation in **D** :

_____

 The Exterior Angle Theorem states that the measure of an _____ angle is equal to the sum of its _____ angles.

REFLECT

3a. Sketch a triangle and draw all of its exterior angles. How many exterior angles does a triangle have at each vertex?

_____

3b. How many total exterior angles does a triangle have?

_____

Find the missing angle measure.

1.

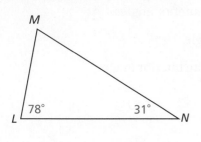

$m\angle M =$ _____

2.

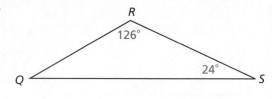

$m\angle Q =$ _____

Use the Triangle Sum Theorem to find the measure of each angle in degrees.

3.

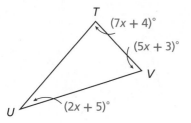

$m\angle T =$ _____

$m\angle U =$ _____

$m\angle V =$ _____

4.

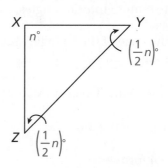

$m\angle X =$ _____

$m\angle Y =$ _____

$m\angle Z =$ _____

Use the Exterior Angles Theorem to find the measure of each angle in degrees.

5.

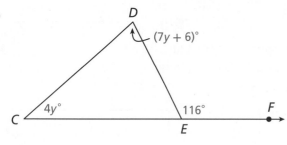

$m\angle C =$ _____

$m\angle D =$ _____

$m\angle DEC =$ _____

6.

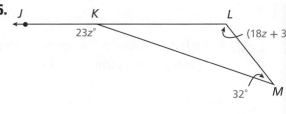

$m\angle L =$ _____

$m\angle MKL =$ _____

$m\angle MKJ =$ _____

Similar Triangles

COMMON CORE

CC.8.G.5

Essential question: *How can you determine when two triangles are similar?*

Recall that similar figures have the same shape, but may have different sizes. Two triangles are similar if their corresponding angles are congruent and the lengths of their corresponding sides are proportional.

1 EXPLORE   Discovering Angle-Angle Similarity

A Use your protractor and a straightedge to draw a triangle. Make one angle measure 45° and another angle measure 60°.

B Compare your triangle to those drawn by your classmates. How are the triangles the same?

_____

How are they different?

_____

C Use the Triangle Sum Theorem to find the measure of the third angle of your triangle.

_____

REFLECT

1a. If two angles in one triangle are congruent to two angles in another triangle, what do you know about the third pair of angles?

_____

_____

1b. Are two pairs of congruent angles enough information to conclude that two triangles are similar? Explain.

_____

_____

> **Angle-Angle (AA) Similarity Postulate**
>
> If two angles of one triangle are congruent to two angles of another triangle, then the triangles are similar.

2 EXAMPLE Using the AA Similarity Postulate

Explain whether the triangles are similar.

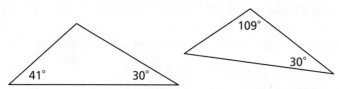

The figure shows only one pair of congruent angles. Find the measure of the third angle in each triangle. Label the angle measures in the figure.

$$41° + 30° + m\angle3 = 180°$$
$$71° + m\angle3 = 180°$$
$$71° + m\angle3 - \boxed{} = 180° - \boxed{}$$
$$m\angle3 = \boxed{}$$

$$\boxed{} + \boxed{} + m\angle3 = 180°$$
$$\boxed{} + m\angle3 = 180°$$
$$\boxed{} + m\angle3 - \boxed{} = 180° - \boxed{}$$
$$m\angle3 = \boxed{}$$

Because _____ in one triangle are congruent to _____
in the other triangle, the triangles are _____.

You can also determine whether two triangles are similar by deciding whether the lengths of the corresponding sides are proportional.

3 EXAMPLE Using Proportional Side Lengths

Explain whether △ABC and △DEF are similar.

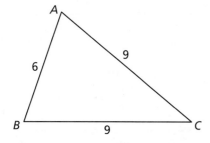
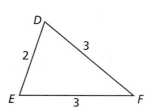

Corresponding parts of triangles are listed in the same order, so $\overline{AB}$

corresponds to $\overline{DE}$, $\overline{BC}$ corresponds to _____, and $\overline{AC}$

corresponds to _____.

Determine whether the lengths of corresponding sides are proportional.

$$\frac{AB}{DE} = \frac{BC}{EF} \quad \rightarrow \quad \frac{6}{\boxed{}} \stackrel{?}{=} \frac{\boxed{}}{\boxed{}} \qquad \textit{Substitute the lengths from the figure.}$$

$$\frac{\boxed{}}{\boxed{}} \stackrel{?}{=} \frac{\boxed{}}{\boxed{}} \qquad \textit{Simplify the ratios.}$$

AC is congruent to BC and DF is congruent to EF, so you do not need to set

up a second proportion. Because the lengths of corresponding sides are

_____, the triangles are _____.

While playing tennis, Matt is 12 meters from the net that is 0.9 meter high. He needs to hit the ball so that it just clears the net and lands 6 meters beyond the base of the net. At what height in meters should Matt hit the tennis ball?

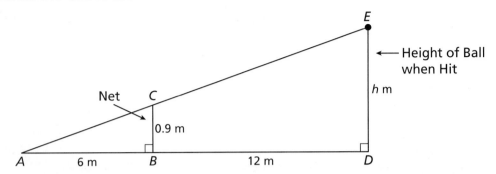

A   Both triangles contain $\angle A$; $\angle A$ in $\triangle ABC$ is congruent to _____ in $\triangle ADE$.

The net $(\overline{BC})$ is perpendicular to the ground $(\overline{AB})$, so $\triangle ABC$ is a right angle. The line representing the height of the ball $(\overline{DE})$ perpendicular to the ground $(\overline{AD})$, so $\angle ADE$ is a _____.

There are two pairs of _____ angles, so $\triangle ABC$ and $\triangle ADE$ are _____.

B   In similar triangles, corresponding side lengths are proportional.

$$\frac{AD}{AB} = \frac{DE}{BC} \quad \rightarrow \quad \frac{6+12}{\boxed{}} = \frac{h}{\boxed{}} \qquad \textit{Substitute the lengths from the figure.}$$

$$\boxed{} \times \frac{18}{\boxed{}} = \frac{h}{\boxed{}} \times \boxed{} \qquad \textit{Use properties of equality to get h by itself.}$$

$$0.9 \times \boxed{} = h \qquad \textit{Simplify.}$$

$$\boxed{} = h \qquad \textit{Multiply.}$$

Matt should hit the ball at a height of _____ meter(s).

TRY THIS!

4.   What if you set up a proportion so that each ratio compares parts of one triangle?

$$\begin{array}{c} \rightarrow \\ \rightarrow \end{array} \frac{BC}{AB} = \frac{DE}{AD} \begin{array}{c} \leftarrow \\ \leftarrow \end{array}$$

Show that this proportion leads to the same value for h as in   **B** .

1. Two transversals intersect two parallel lines as shown. Explain whether △*ABC* and △*DEC* are similar.

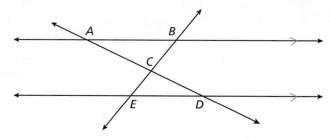

_____

_____

_____

_____

2. A flagpole casts a shadow 23.5 feet long. At the same time of day, Mrs. Gilbert, who is 5.5 feet tall, casts a shadow that is 7.5 feet long. How tall in feet is the flagpole? Round your answer to the tenths place.

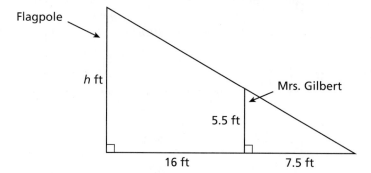

3. △*LMN* and △*QRS* are similar. Find the value of *x*.

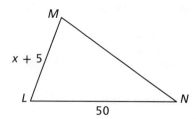
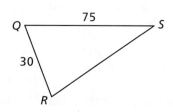

Similar Triangles and Slope

COMMON
CORE

CC.8.EE.6

Essential question: *How can you show that the slope of a line is the same between any two points on the line?*

1 **EXPLORE** **Investigating Slope**

The graph shows the linear function $y = -\frac{2}{3}x + 4$.

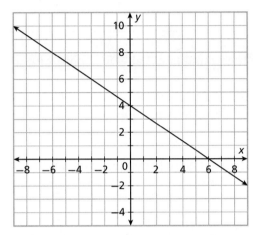

A Find the slope of the line using the points $(0, 4)$ and $(-3, 6)$.

$$m = \frac{6 - \boxed{}}{\boxed{} - 0} = \frac{\boxed{}}{\boxed{}} = \boxed{}$$

B Find the slope of the line using a different pair of points on the line.

_____

C Find the slope of the line using another pair of points on the line.

_____

REFLECT

1a. What does slope represent?

_____

1b. Does it matter which pair of points you use when finding the slope of a line? Explain.

_____

_____

Use similar triangles to show that the slope of a line is constant.
Use this space to make your drawing:

A Draw line ℓ that is not a horizontal line. Label four points on the line as A, B, C, and D.

You need to show that the slope between points A and B is the same as the slope between points C and D.

B Draw the rise and run for the slope between points A and B. Label the intersection as point E. Draw the rise and run for the slope between points C and D. Label the intersection as point F.

C Write expressions for the slope between A and B and between C and D.

Slope between A and B: $\dfrac{BE}{\boxed{}}$ Slope between C and D: $\dfrac{\boxed{}}{CF}$

D Extend $\overleftrightarrow{AE}$ and $\overleftrightarrow{CF}$ across your drawing. $\overleftrightarrow{AE}$ and $\overleftrightarrow{CF}$ are both horizontal lines, so they are parallel. Line ℓ is a transversal that intersects parallel lines.

E Complete the following statements:

$\angle BAE$ and _____ are corresponding angles and are _____.

$\angle BEA$ and _____ are right angles and are _____.

F By Angle-Angle Similarity, $\triangle ABE$ and _____ are similar triangles.

G Use the fact that the lengths of corresponding sides of similar triangles are proportional to complete the following ratios: $\dfrac{BE}{DF} = \dfrac{\boxed{}}{CF}$.

H Recall that you can also write the proportion so that the ratios compare parts of the same triangle: $\dfrac{\boxed{}}{AE} = \dfrac{DF}{\boxed{}}$.

I The proportion you wrote in step **H** shows that the ratios you wrote in **C** are equal. So, the slope of the line is constant.

Using the Pythagorean Theorem

COMMON
CORE

CC.8.G.7
CC.8.G.8

Essential question: *How can you use the Pythagorean Theorem to solve problems?*

In a right triangle, the two sides that form the right angle are the **legs**. The side opposite the right angle is the **hypotenuse**.

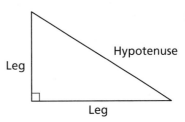

The Pythagorean Theorem

In a right triangle, the sum of the squares of the lengths of the legs is equal to the square of the length of the hypotenuse.

If a and b are legs and c is the hypotenuse, $a^2 + b^2 = c^2$.

1 **EXAMPLE** **Using the Pythagorean Theorem**

Find the length of the missing side.

A

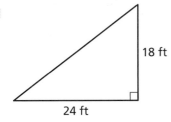

18 ft

24 ft

$$a^2 + b^2 = c^2$$

$24^2 + \boxed{}^2 = c^2$ *Substitute into the formula.*

$\boxed{} + \boxed{} = c^2$ *Simplify.*

$\boxed{} = c^2$ *Add.*

$\boxed{} = c$ *Take the square root of both sides.*

The length of the hypotenuse is _____ ft.

B

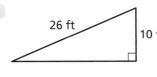

26 ft

10 ft

$$a^2 + b^2 = c^2$$

$a^2 + \boxed{}^2 = 26^2$ *Substitute into the formula.*

$a^2 + \boxed{} = 676$ *Simplify.*

$a^2 = \boxed{}$ *Use properties of equality to get a^2 by itself.*

$a = \boxed{}$ *Take the square root of both sides.*

The length of the leg is _____ cm.

REFLECT

1. If you are given the length of the hypotenuse and one leg, does it matter whether you solve for a or b? Explain.

_____

_____

Approximate the length of the hypotenuse to the nearest tenth without using a calculator.

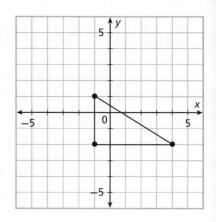

Find the length of the vertical leg: _____ units

Find the length of the horizontal leg: _____ units

$$a^2 + b^2 = c^2$$

$\boxed{}^2 + \boxed{}^2 = c^2$ *Substitute into the formula.*

$\boxed{} + \boxed{} = c^2$ *Simplify.*

$\boxed{} = c^2$ *Add.*

$\sqrt{\boxed{}} = c$ *Take the square root of both sides.*

$\sqrt{\boxed{}}$ is between _____ and _____, so $\sqrt{\boxed{}} \approx \boxed{}$.

The hypotenuse is about _____ units long.

TRY THIS!

2a. Approximate the length of the hypotenuse to the nearest tenth without using a calculator.

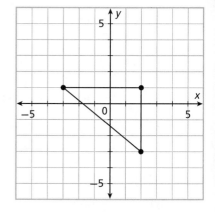

REFLECT

2b. Which side of a right triangle is always the longest side?

_____

2c. How could you find the length of the legs of an isosceles right triangle if you are only given the length of the hypotenuse?

_____

_____

2d. **Conjecture** Explain whether the lengths 2 cm, 3 cm, and 7 cm could be the side lengths of a right triangle.

_____

_____

_____

Mr. Woo wants to ship a fishing rod that is 42 inches long to his son. He has a box that measures 10 inches by 10 inches by 40 inches. Will the fishing rod fit in the box?

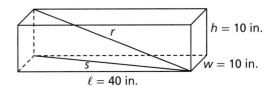

$h = 10$ in.

$w = 10$ in.

$\ell = 40$ in.

r

s

<u>Will the rod fit in the bottom of the box?</u>

Let s represent the length of the diagonal across the bottom of the box.

$$w^2 + \ell^2 = s^2$$

$$10^2 + \boxed{}^2 = s^2 \qquad \textit{Substitute into the formula.}$$

$$\boxed{} + \boxed{} = s^2 \qquad \textit{Simplify.}$$

$$\boxed{} = s^2 \qquad \textit{Add.}$$

$$\sqrt{\boxed{}} = s \qquad \textit{Take the square root of both sides.}$$

$$\boxed{} \approx s \qquad \textit{Use a calculator to round to the nearest tenth.}$$

<u>Will the rod fit diagonally from one bottom corner to the opposite top corner?</u>

Let r represent the length from a bottom corner to the opposite top corner.

$$h^2 + s^2 = r^2$$

$$\boxed{}^2 + \sqrt{\boxed{}^2} = r^2 \qquad \textit{Substitute into the formula. Use the value for } s^2.$$

$$\boxed{} + \boxed{} = r^2 \qquad \textit{Simplify.}$$

$$\boxed{} = r^2 \qquad \textit{Add.}$$

$$\sqrt{\boxed{}} = r \qquad \textit{Take the square root of both sides.}$$

$$\boxed{} \approx r \qquad \textit{Use a calculator to round to the nearest tenth.}$$

Explain whether the rod will fit in the box. If so, tell how.

_____

_____

TRY THIS!

3. Tina ordered a replacement part for her desk. It was shipped in a box that measures 4 in. by 4 in. by 14 in. What is the greatest length in whole inches that the part could have been?

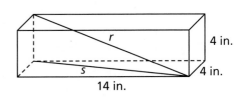

r

s

4 in.

4 in.

14 in.

Find the length of the missing side. Approximate square roots of non-perfect squares to the nearest tenth without using a calculator.

1.

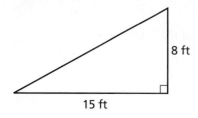

8 ft

15 ft

_____

2.

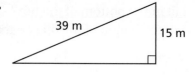

39 m

15 m

_____

3.

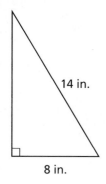

14 in.

8 in.

_____

4.

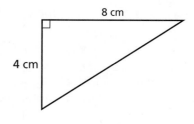

8 cm

4 cm

_____

Approximate the length of the hypotenuse to the nearest tenth without using a calculator.

5.

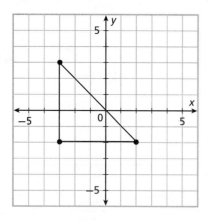

_____

6.

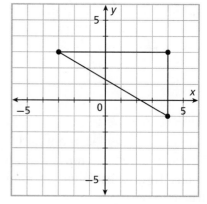

_____

7. What is the longest flagpole (in whole feet) that could be shipped in a box that measures 1 ft by 2 ft by 12 ft?

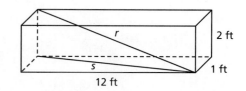

r

2 ft

s

1 ft

12 ft

_____

5-6

Proving the Pythagorean Theorem

Essential question: *How can you prove the Pythagorean Theorem and its converse?*

COMMON
CORE

CC.8.G.6

---

1 **EXPLORE**   **Using Area to Prove the Pythagorean Theorem**

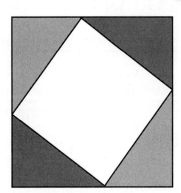

A Draw a right triangle on a piece of paper and cut it out. Make one leg shorter than the other.

B Trace your triangle onto another piece of paper four times, arranging them as shown. For each triangle, label the shorter leg *a*, the longer leg *b*, and the hypotenuse *c*.

C What is the area of the unshaded square?

_____

Label the unshaded square with its area.

D Trace your original triangle onto a piece of paper four times again, arranging them as shown. Draw a line outlining a larger square that is the same size as the figure you made in **B** .

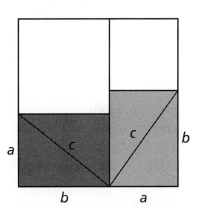

E What is the area of the unshaded square at the top right of the figure in **D** ? at the top left?

_____

Label the unshaded squares with their areas.

F What is the total area of the unshaded regions of the figure in **D** ?

_____

_____

REFLECT

1a. Explain whether the figures in **B** and **D** have the same area.

_____

1b. Explain whether the unshaded regions of the figures in **B** and **D** have the same area.

_____

_____

_____

1c. Write an equation relating the area of the unshaded region in step B to the unshaded region in **D** .

_____

The Pythagorean Theorem says "If a triangle is a right triangle, then $a^2 + b^2 = c^2$."

The *converse* of the Pythagorean Theorem says "If $a^2 + b^2 = c^2$, then the triangle is a right triangle."

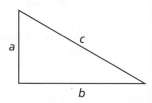

2 EXPLORE   **Testing the Converse of the Pythagorean Theorem**

Decide whether the converse of the Pythagorean Theorem is true.

A   Verify that the following sets of lengths make the equation $a^2 + b^2 = c^2$ is true. Record your results in the table.

a	b	c	Is $a^2 + b^2 = c^2$ true?	Makes a right triangle?
3	4	5		
5	12	13		
7	24	25		
8	15	17		
20	21	29		

B   For each set of lengths in the table, cut strips of grid paper with a width of one square and lengths that correspond to the values of a, b, and c.

C   For each set of lengths, use the strips of grid paper to try to form a right triangle. An example using the first set of lengths is shown here.

Record your findings in the table.

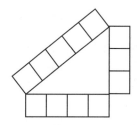

REFLECT

2.   Based on your observations, explain whether you think the converse of the Pythagorean Theorem is true.

_____

_____

_____

Volume Formulas

Essential question: *How can you solve problems using the formulas for volume?*

COMMON CORE

CC.8.G.9

A cylinder has two parallel congruent circular bases. The area of a base is πr^2.

Volume of a Cylinder

The volume of a cylinder with base area
B, radius r, and height h is $V = Bh$,
or $V = \pi r^2 h$.

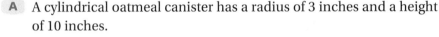

1 **EXAMPLE** **Volume of a Cylinder**

**Find the volume of each cylinder. Round your answers to the nearest
tenth if necessary. Use 3.14 for π.**

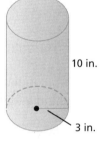

A A cylindrical oatmeal canister has a radius of 3 inches and a height
of 10 inches.

$V = \pi r^2 h$

$\approx 3.14 \cdot \boxed{}^2 \cdot \boxed{}$ *Substitute into the formula.*

$\approx 3.14 \cdot \boxed{} \cdot \boxed{}$ *Simplify the exponent.*

$\approx \boxed{}$ in^3 *Multiply.*

10 in.

3 in.

The volume of the canister is about _____ in^3.

B A drink can has a diameter of 6.4 centimeters and a height
of 13 centimeters.

First, find the radius: _____ cm.

$V = \pi r^2 h$

$\approx 3.14 \cdot \boxed{}^2 \cdot \boxed{}$ *Substitute into the formula.*

$\approx 3.14 \cdot \boxed{} \cdot \boxed{}$ *Simplify the exponent.*

$\approx \boxed{}$ cm^3 *Multiply.*

13 cm

6.4 cm

The volume of the can is about _____ cm^3.

TRY THIS!

1a. The top layer of a wedding cake has a diameter of
10 inches and a height of 6 inches. Find the volume of the
top layer of the cake. Round your answer to the nearest
tenth if necessary. Use 3.14 for π.

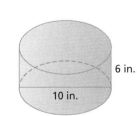

6 in.

10 in.

_____

A cone has one circular base. The area of the base is πr^2.

Volume of a Cone

The volume of a cone with base area B, radius r, and height h is $V = \frac{1}{3}Bh$, or $V = \frac{1}{3}\pi r^2 h$.

2 **EXAMPLE** Volume of a Cone

Find the volume of each cone. Round your answers to the nearest tenth if necessary. Use 3.14 for π.

A A candle in the shape of a cone has a height of 8 inches and a radius of 2 inches.

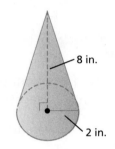

8 in.

2 in.

$V = \frac{1}{3}\pi r^2 h$

$\approx \frac{1}{3} \cdot 3.14 \cdot \boxed{}^2 \cdot \boxed{}$ *Substitute into the formula.*

$\approx \frac{1}{3} \cdot 3.14 \cdot \boxed{} \cdot \boxed{}$ *Simplify the exponent.*

$\approx \boxed{}$ in^3 *Multiply.*

The volume of the candle is about _____ in^3.

B Jacob has a tent that is cone-shaped. It has a height of 9 feet and a diameter of 8 feet.

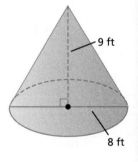

9 ft

8 ft

First, find the radius: _____ ft.

$V = \frac{1}{3}\pi r^2 h$

$\approx \frac{1}{3} \cdot 3.14 \cdot \boxed{}^2 \cdot \boxed{}$ *Substitute into the formula.*

$\approx \frac{1}{3} \cdot 3.14 \cdot \boxed{} \cdot \boxed{}$ *Simplify the exponent.*

$\approx \boxed{}$ ft^3 *Multiply.*

The volume of the tent is about _____ ft^3.

TRY THIS!

2a. A cone has a diameter of 6 centimeters and a height of 11.5 centimeters. Find the volume of the cone. Round your answer to the nearest tenth if necessary. Use 3.14 for π.

_____

REFLECT

2b. What is the relationship between the volume of a cylinder and a cone with the same height and same radius?

_____

All the points in a sphere are the same distance from the center of the sphere.

Volume of a Sphere

The volume of a sphere
with radius r is $V = \frac{4}{3}\pi r^3$.

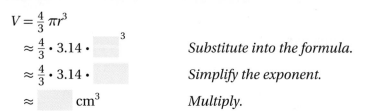

3 **EXAMPLE** Volume of a Sphere

Find the volume of each sphere. Round your answers to the nearest tenth if necessary. Use 3.14 for π.

A The radius of a golf ball is 2.1 centimeters.

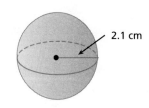
2.1 cm

$V = \frac{4}{3}\pi r^3$

$\approx \frac{4}{3} \cdot 3.14 \cdot \boxed{}^3$ *Substitute into the formula.*

$\approx \frac{4}{3} \cdot 3.14 \cdot \boxed{}$ *Simplify the exponent.*

$\approx \boxed{}$ cm^3 *Multiply.*

The volume of a golf ball is about _____ cm^3.

B The diameter of a tennis ball is 7 centimeters.

First, find the radius: _____ cm.

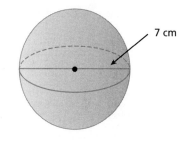
7 cm

$V = \frac{4}{3}\pi r^3$

$\approx \frac{4}{3} \cdot 3.14 \cdot \boxed{}^3$ *Substitute into the formula.*

$\approx \frac{4}{3} \cdot 3.14 \cdot \boxed{}$ *Simplify the exponent.*

$\approx \boxed{}$ cm^3 *Multiply.*

The volume of the tent is about _____ cm^3.

TRY THIS!

3a. A baseball has a diameter of 2.9 inches. Find the volume of the baseball. Round your answer to the nearest tenth if necessary. Use 3.14 for π.

_____

REFLECT

3b. A hemisphere is half of a sphere. Explain how you would find the volume of a hemisphere.

_____

_____

Find the volume of each figure. Round your answers to the nearest tenth if necessary. Use 3.14 for π.

1.

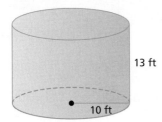

13 ft

10 ft

2.

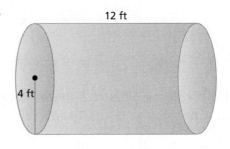

12 ft

4 ft

_____

_____

3. A cylinder has a radius of 4 centimeters and height of 40 centimeters.

_____

4. A cylinder has a radius of 8 meters and height of 4 meters.

_____

5.

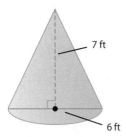

7 ft

6 ft

6.

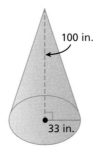

100 in.

33 in.

_____

_____

7. A sphere has a radius of 3.1 meters.

_____

8. A sphere has a diameter of 18 inches.

_____

9. A farmer stores corn in a silo that is in the shape of a cylinder with a hemisphere on top. The diameter of the silo is 30 feet, and the total height of the silo is 60 feet.

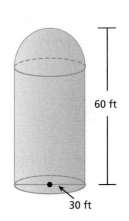

60 ft

30 ft

   a. Find the radius of the hemisphere. _____

   b. Find the height of the cylinder. _____

   c. Find the volume of the cylinder. _____

   d. Find the volume of the hemisphere. _____

   e. Find the volume of the silo. _____

Problem Solving Connections

Where in the Park is Xander? Xander plans a hiking trip in a national park. Instead of obtaining an accurate trail map from the National Park Service, he downloaded *Bob's Hiking Guide* from a website. Xander's hiking guide eventually gets him lost. Can you help find Xander?

COMMON CORE

CC.8.G.5
CC.8.G.6
CC.8.G.7
CC.8.G.8
CC.8.G.9
CC.8.EE.6

1 | Packing for the Trip

Xander fills his backpack with his hiking guide, a book of matches, a flashlight, and two bottles of water. General guidelines suggest that a person drink at least eight 8-oz servings of water per day. Depending on a person's activity level, their body may require more water.

A Xander plans to be hiking for most of the day, so hiking resources suggest that he have at least 3 liters of water with him. The bottles he brought with him are cylinders with a radius of 3 cm and a height of 30 cm. What is the volume of one bottle in cubic centimeters?

B One cubic centimeter has the same volume as one milliliter. There are 1000 milliliters in 1 liter. Does Xander have enough water with him?

C One milliliter has the same volume as about 0.034 fluid ounces. Does Xander have at least eight 8-oz servings of water packed?

2 Following the Map

Xander follows the maps in *Bob's Hiking Guide* and starts out on South Springs Trail.

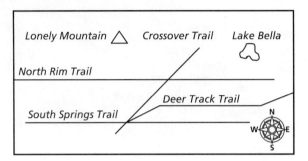

A Xander wants to take Crossover Trail northeast to intersect with North Rim Trail. A note on Xander's map reads:

> "There are a bunch of trails that split off from the intersection of South Springs Trail and Crossover Trail. I didn't draw them all on my map. But I know North Rim Trail and South Springs Trail run parallel and that the angle in the southeast corner of North Rim Trail and Crossover Trail measures 120°. Good Luck! —Bob"

When Xander gets to the intersection of South Springs Trail and Crossover Trail, the only signs on the four trails he sees are given in degrees. How can Xander determine which trail to take when he gets to the intersection of South Springs and Crossover Trail?

_____

_____

_____

_____

_____

Trail A
15°

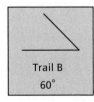

Trail B
60°

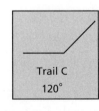

Trail C
120°

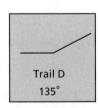

Trail D
135°

B The trail markers at the intersection of South Springs Trail and Crossover Trail are the ones below. Which trail should Xander take?

_____

_____

3 Finding a Landmark

Xander makes a mistake and takes the trail marked 60°. After hiking for a while, he realizes that he is lost and his cell phone battery is almost dead.

A Xander stands 50 feet in front of a young tree and looks up across the top of the tree to the top of a mountain in the distance. Xander estimates the height of the tree as 15 feet. Draw a diagram involving similar triangles that shows the relationship between the tree and the mountain from Xander's perspective.

B Explain how you know that the triangles in your diagram are similar triangles.

C How can the diagram help Xander?

4 Finding Xander

Xander's cell phone battery has just enough life to make a brief call to 911. He quickly tells the dispatcher about the mountain and the tree. The dispatcher tells Xander to stay in the same spot and then Xander's phone dies.

A The dispatcher contacts a ranger at the National Park Service. The ranger knows that the height of the mountain is 3000 feet. Use the height of the mountain and your diagram to find Xander's distance from the mountain.

Xander is about _____ feet from the mountain.

Xander did not mention a lake or waterfall, but did mention being near trees. The ranger uses his knowledge of the park to assume that Xander is south of the mountain. He contacts ranger stations in that area of the park and tells them to look for signs of a lost hiker.

B Xander makes a fire while he waits for rescue. The fire is spotted by two park rangers in towers that are 2000 feet apart. The rangers use the line between the towers as the base of a triangle and determine that the angle to the fire from each tower measures 45°.

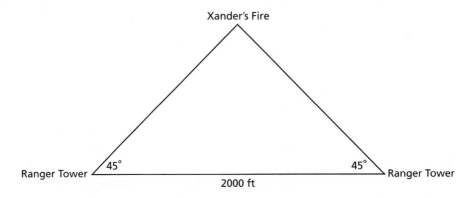

C Classify the triangle as acute, right, or obtuse. Explain how you know.

_____

_____

_____

D When two angles in a triangle have the same measure, the sides opposite those angles have the same length. How can you find the lengths of the missing sides?

_____

_____

E Find Xander's distance from the ranger towers.

Xander is about _____ feet from either ranger tower.

Name _____ Class _____ Date _____

MULTIPLE CHOICE

1. What is the measure of angle *x*?

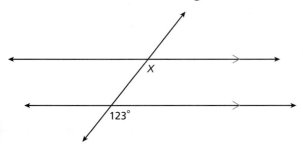

A. 57°

C. 123°

B. 66°

D. 180°

2. What is the value of *x*?

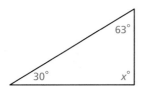

F. 30°

H. 87°

G. 63°

J. 93°

3. Tim works for a tree-trimming company and needs to know the height of a pine tree. Tim, who is 6 feet tall, casts a shadow that is 8 feet long at the same time that the tree casts a shadow that is 32 feet long. What is the height of the tree?

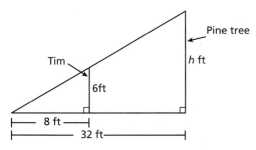

A. 18 feet

C. 42.7 feet

B. 24 feet

D. 48 feet

4. One of the sails of a sailboat is in the shape of a right triangle. What is the height of the sail?

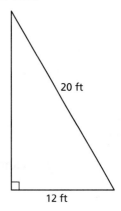

F. 16 feet

H. 32 feet

G. 23.3 feet

J. 64 feet

5. The table gives the side lengths for four triangles. Which of the triangles is a right triangle?

Triangle	Length of Sides
A	7, 9, 12
B	12, 13, 14
C	10, 23, 25
D	15, 20, 25

A. Triangle A

B. Triangle B

C. Triangle C

D. Triangle D

6. What is the approximate volume of a cone with a height of 4 inches and a radius of 2 inches?

F. 8.4 cubic inches

G. 16.7 cubic inches

H. 25.1 cubic inches

J. 50.2 cubic inches

7. What is the approximate volume of the cylinder?

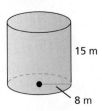

15 m

8 m

A. 376.8 cubic meters

B. 753.6 cubic meters

C. 3014.4 cubic meters

D. 5652.0 cubic meters

FREE RESPONSE

8. A 13-foot-long ladder leans against the side of a building. The bottom of the ladder is 5 feet from the base of the building. What height does the ladder reach?

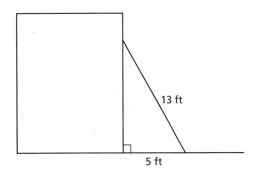

13 ft

5 ft

9. A great circle divides a sphere into two hemispheres. For a men's regulation basketball, the circumference of a great circle is 29.5 inches. Show how to find the volume of the basketball.

Use the figure for 10–11.

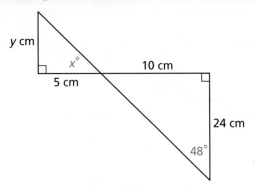

y cm

$x°$

10 cm

5 cm

24 cm

48°

10. Explain how to find the value of x.

_____

_____

_____

_____

11. Explain how to find the value of y.

_____

_____

_____

12. A small waffle cone has a height of 6 inches and a diameter of 2.5 inches. A large waffle cone has a height of 7.25 inches and a diameter of 3.25 inches. Show how to find the difference in the volumes.

Statistics and Probability

Unit Focus

You have worked with one-variable statistics, and now you will expand your statistics skills to bivariate, or two-variable, statistics. You will use scatter plots to analyze the relationship, or association, between two quantities and be able to recognize outliers and clusters. You will use two-way tables to find relative frequencies and determine if there is an association between two variables.

Unit at a Glance

COMMON CORE

Lesson	Standards for Mathematical Content
6-1 Scatter Plots and Association	CC.8.SP.1
6-2 Scatter Plots and Predictions	CC.8.SP.2, CC.8.SP.3
6-3 Two-Way Tables	CC.8.SP.4
Problem Solving Connections	
Test Prep	

UNIT 6

Unpacking the Common Core State Standards

Use the table to help you understand the Common Core State Standards that are taught in this unit. Refer to the lessons listed after each standard for exploration and practice.

COMMON CORE Standards for Mathematical Content	What It Means For You
CC.8.SP.1 Construct and interpret scatter plots for bivariate measurement data to investigate patterns of association between two quantities. Describe patterns such as clustering, outliers, positive or negative association, linear association, and nonlinear association. Lesson 6-1	You will make and interpret scatter plots. You will describe patterns in two-variable data including trends, clusters, outliers, and association.
CC.8.SP.2 Know that straight lines are widely used to model relationships between two quantitative variables. For scatter plots that suggest a linear association, informally fit a straight line, and informally assess the model fit by judging the closeness of the data points to the line. Lesson 6-2	You will draw a trend line to model data displayed in a scatter plot. You will use that line to make predictions.
CC.8.SP.3 Use the equation of a linear model to solve problems in the context of bivariate measurement data, interpreting the slope and intercept. Lesson 6-2	You will write an equation for a trend line that models two-variable data. You will interpret the slope of the line and y-intercept and use the equation for the line to make predictions.
CC.8.SP.4 Understand that patterns of association can also be seen in bivariate categorical data by displaying frequencies and relative frequencies in a two-way table. Construct and interpret a two-way table summarizing data on two categorical variables collected from the same subjects. Use relative frequencies calculated for rows or columns to describe possible association between the two variables. Lesson 6-3	You will use two-way tables to organize data and calculate relative frequencies. You will use relative frequencies to describe possible associations between two variables or events.

UNIT 6

Scatter Plots and Association

COMMON CORE

CC.8.SP.1

Essential question: *How can you construct and interpret scatter plots?*

A set of **bivariate data** involves two variables. Bivariate data are used to explore the relationship between two variables. You can graph bivariate data on a *scatter plot*. A **scatter plot** is a graph with points plotted to show the relationship between two sets of data.

1 **EXPLORE**   **Making a Scatter Plot**

The final question on a math test reads, "How many hours did you spend studying for this test?" The teacher records the number of hours each student studied and the grade the student received on the test.

Hours Spent Studying	Test Grade
0	75
0.5	80
1	80
1	85
1.5	85
1.5	95
2	90
3	100
4	90

A Make a prediction about the relationship between the number of hours spent studying and test grades.

_____

_____

_____

B Make a scatter plot. Graph hours spent studying as the independent variable and test grade as the dependent variable.

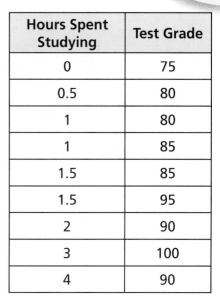

REFLECT

1a. What trend do you see in the data?

_____

_____

_____

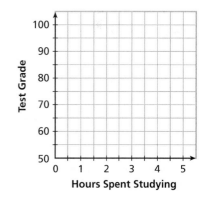

1b. Do you think that studying for 10 hours would greatly increase a student's grade?

_____

_____

1c. Why might a student who studied fewer hours make a higher score?

_____

_____

A **cluster** is a set of closely grouped data. Data may cluster around a point or along a line. An **outlier** is a data point that is very different from the rest of the data in the set.

2 **EXAMPLE** **Interpreting Clusters and Outliers**

A scientist gathers information about the eruptions of Old Faithful, a geyser in Yellowstone National Park. She uses the data to create a scatter plot. The data shows the length of time between eruptions (interval) and how long the eruption lasts (duration).

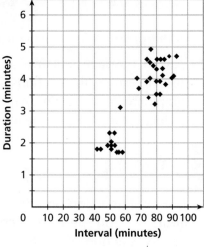

A Describe any clusters you see in the scatter plot.

_____

_____

B What do the clusters tell you about eruptions of Old Faithful?

_____

_____

C Describe any outliers you see in the scatter plot.

_____

_____

REFLECT

2a. Suppose the geyser erupts for 2.2 minutes after a 75-minute interval. Would this point lie in one of the clusters? Would it be an outlier? Explain your answer.

_____

_____

_____

_____

2b. Suppose the geyser erupts after an 80-minute interval. Give a range of possible duration times for which the point on the scatter plot would not be considered an outlier. Give your reasoning.

_____

_____

_____

_____

Association tells you how sets of data are related. A positive association means that both data sets increase together. A negative association means that as one data set increases, the other decreases. No association means that changes in one data set do not affect the other data set.

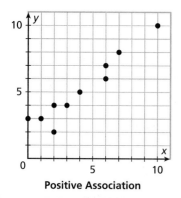

Positive Association

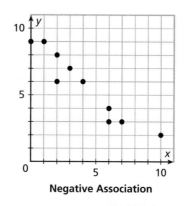

Negative Association

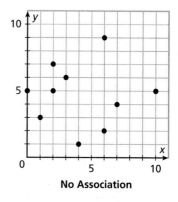

No Association

When data shows a positive or negative association and falls along a line, there is a linear association. When data shows a positive or negative relationship, but does not fall along a line, there is a nonlinear association.

3 EXPLORE   **Determining Association**

Susan surveyed 20 people about the price of a cleaning product she developed. She asked each person whether they would buy the cleaner at different prices. A person may answer yes or no to more than one price. Susan's results are shown in the table.

Price ($)	Buyers
2	20
4	19
6	17
8	13
10	8
12	2

A Make a scatter plot of the data.

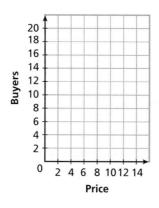

B Describe the type(s) of association you see between price and number of people who would buy at that price. Explain.

_____

_____

_____

Bob recorded his height at different ages.

Age (years)	6	8	10	12	14
Height (inches)	45	50	55	61	63

1. Make a scatter plot of Bob's data.

2. Describe the type(s) of association between Bob's age and his height. Explain.

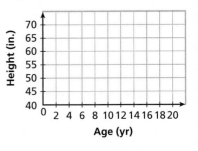

_____

_____

_____

_____

_____

Ms. Banks recorded the height and reading level of several students.

3. Describe the type(s) of association between a student's height and his or her reading level. Explain.

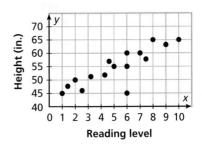

_____

_____

_____

_____

_____

4. **Error Analysis** Ms. Banks concludes that an increase in reading level causes an increase in height. Explain whether you agree with her conclusion.

_____

_____

_____

5. Add a point that is an outlier to the graph. Then, explain why it is an outlier.

_____

_____

Scatter Plots and Predictions

COMMON CORE

CC.8.SP.2
CC.8.SP.3

Essential question: *How can you use a trend line to make a prediction from a scatter plot?*

When a scatter plot shows a linear association, you can use a line to model the relationship between the variables. A **trend line** is a straight line that comes closest to the points on a scatter plot.

1 EXPLORE   Drawing a Trend Line

Joyce is training for a 10K race. For some of her training runs, she records the distance she ran and how many minutes she ran.

Distance (mi)	Time (min)
4	38
2	25
1	7
2	16
3	26
5	55
2	20
4	45
3	31

A   Make a scatter plot of Joyce's running data.

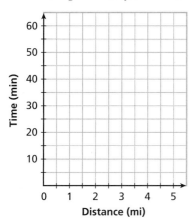

B   To draw a trend line, use a straight edge to draw a line that has about the same number of points above and below it. Ignore any outliers.

C   Use your trend line to predict how long it would take Joyce to run 4.5 miles.

_____

REFLECT

1a. How well does your trend line fit the data?

_____

_____

1b. Do you think you can use a scatter plot that shows no association to make a prediction? Explain your answer.

_____

_____

The scatter plot shows the relationship between the number of chapters and the total number of pages for several books. Draw a trend line, write an equation for the trend line, and describe the meanings of the slope and *y*-intercept.

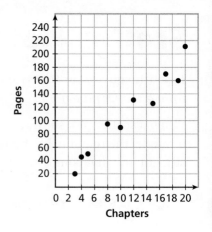

Pages / Chapters

A Draw a trend line. It will be easier to write an equation for the line if it goes through two of the data points. (Hint: Use (5, 50) as one of the points.)

Identify another point that the trend line goes through:

$\left(\boxed{}, \boxed{}\right).$

B What type(s) of association does the scatter plot show?

_____

C Do you expect the slope of the line to be positive or negative?

_____

D Find the slope of the trend line.

$$m = \frac{\boxed{} - 50}{\boxed{} - 5} = \frac{\boxed{}}{\boxed{}} = \boxed{}$$

E Use the equation $y = mx + b$, the slope, and the point (5, 50). Substitute values for y, m, and x into the equation and solve for b.

$y = mx + b$

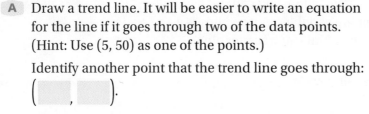

$\boxed{} = \boxed{} \cdot \boxed{} + b$ *Substitute for y, m, and b.*

$\boxed{} = \boxed{} + b$ *Simplify on the right side.*

$\boxed{} = \boxed{} + b$ *Subtract the number that is added to b from both sides.*

$-\frac{\boxed{}}{} \quad -\frac{\boxed{}}{}$

$\boxed{} = b$

Use your slope and *y*-intercept values to write an equation in slope-intercept form.

$y = \boxed{} \, x + \boxed{}$

F What is the meaning of the slope in this situation?

_____

_____

G What is the meaning of the *y*-intercept in this situation?

_____

When you use a trend line or its equation to predict a value between data points that you already know, you *interpolate* the predicted value. When you make a prediction that is outside the data that you know, you *extrapolate* the predicted value.

3 EXPLORE Making Predictions

Refer to the scatter plot and trend line in **2**.

A Use the equation of the trend line to predict how many pages would be in a book with 26 chapters.

Is this prediction an example of interpolation or extrapolation?

_____

$y =$ ⬚   *Write the equation for your trend line.*

$y =$ ⬚   *Substitute the number of chapters for x.*

$y =$ ⬚   *Simplify.*

I predict that a book with 26 chapters would have _____ pages.

B Use the equation of the trend line to predict how many pages would be in a book with 14 chapters.

Is this prediction an example of interpolation or extrapolation?

_____

$y =$ ⬚   *Write the equation for your trend line.*

$y =$ ⬚   *Substitute the number of chapters for x.*

$y =$ ⬚   *Simplify.*

I predict that a book with 14 chapters would have _____ pages.

REFLECT

3a. How well do your new points fit the original data?

_____

3b. Do you think that extrapolation or interpolation is more accurate? Explain.

_____

_____

_____

_____

Angela recorded the price of different number of ounces of bulk grains. She made a scatter plot of her data. Use the scatter plot for 1–5.

1. Draw a trend line for the scatter plot.

2. How do you know whether your trend line is a good fit for the data?

   _____

   _____

   _____

   _____

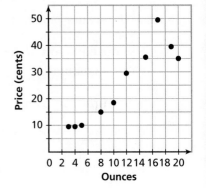

3. Write an equation for your trend line. _____

4. Use the equation for your trend line to interpolate the price of 7 ounces.

   _____

5. Use the equation for your trend line to extrapolate the price of 50 ounces.

   _____

6. A scatter plot shows the relationship between a baby's length and age. Why might an extrapolated data point not be very accurate?

   _____

   _____

   _____

7. **Error Analysis** Carl graphed the data shown in the scatter plot and then drew a trend line. Why is a trend line not a good fit for this data?

   _____

   _____

   _____

   _____

   _____

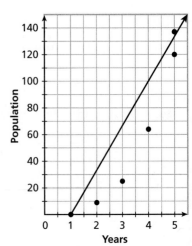

Two-Way Tables

COMMON
CORE

CC.8.SP.4

Essential question: *How can you construct and interpret two-way tables?*

The **frequency** is the number of times an event occurs. A **two-way table** shows the frequencies of data that is categorized two ways. The rows indicate one categorization and the columns indicate another.

1 EXPLORE Making a Two-Way Table

A poll of 120 town residents found that 40% own a bike. Of those who own a bike, 75% shop at the town's farmer's market. Of those who do not own a bike, 25% shop at the town's farmer's market.

	Farmer's Market	No Farmer's Market	TOTAL
Bike			
No Bike			
TOTAL			

A Start in the bottom right cell of the table. Enter the total number of people polled.

B **Fill in the right column.** 40% of those polled own a bike.

40% of 120 is _____.

The remaining people polled do not own a bike. The number who do not own a bike is 120 − _____ = _____.

C **Fill in the top row.** 75% of those who own a bike also shop at the market.

75% of _____ is _____.

The remaining bike owners do not shop at the market. The number of bike owners who do not shop at the market is _____.

D **Fill in the second row.** 25% of those who do not own a bike shop at the market.

25% of _____ is _____.

The remaining people without bikes do not shop at the market. The number without a bike who do not shop at the market is _____.

E **Fill in the last row.** In each column, add the numbers in the first two rows to find the total number of people who shop at the farmer's market and who do not shop at the farmer's market.

F What percent of all the residents polled shop at the farmer's market?

$$\frac{}{120} = $$

_____% of people polled shop at the farmer's market.

> REFLECT

1. How can you check that your table is completed correctly?

_____

_____

Relative frequency is the ratio of the number of times an event occurs to the total number of events. In **1**, the relative frequency of bike owners who shop at the market is $\frac{36}{120} = 0.30 = 30\%$. You can use relative frequencies to decide if there is an association between two variables or events.

2 **E X A M P L E**   **Deciding Whether There Is an Association**

Determine whether there is an association between the events.

A One hundred teens were polled about whether they are required to do chores and whether they have a curfew. Is there an association between having a curfew and having to do chores?

	Curfew	No Curfew	TOTAL
Chores	16	4	20
No Chores	16	64	80
TOTAL	32	68	100

Find the relative frequency of having to do chores.

Total who have to do chores → $\dfrac{}{100} = = $ %
Total number of teens polled →

Find the relative frequency of having to do chores among those who have a curfew.

Number with a curfew who have to do chores → $\dfrac{}{32} = = $ %
Total number with a curfew →

Compare the relative frequencies. Students who have a curfew are less likely/more likely to have to do chores than the general population.

Is there an association between having a curfew and having to do chores? Explain.

_____

_____

B Data from 200 flights was collected. The flights were categorized as domestic or international and late or not late. Is there an association between international flights and a flight being late?

	Late	Not Late	TOTAL
Domestic	30	120	150
International	10	40	50
TOTAL	40	160	200

Find the relative frequency of a flight being late.

Total flights that are late →
Total number of flights → $\dfrac{}{} = = $ %

Find the relative frequency of a flight being late among international flights.

Number of international flights that are late →
Total number of international flights → $\dfrac{}{} = = $ %

Compare the relative frequencies. International flights are less likely / equally likely / more likely to be late than flights in general.

Is there an association between international flights and a flight being late? Explain.

_____

_____

REFLECT

3a. Compare the relative frequency of having a curfew and having chores to the relative frequency of not having a curfew and having chores. Does this comparison help you draw a conclusion about whether there is an association between having a curfew and having chores? Explain.

_____

_____

_____

3b. Compare the relative frequency of domestic flights being late to the relative frequency of international flights being late. Does this comparison help you draw a conclusion about whether there is an association between international flights and being late? Explain.

_____

_____

_____

Karen asked 150 students at her school if they played sports. She also recorded whether the student was a boy or girl. Of the 150 students, 20% did not play sports, 60% of the total were girls, and 70% of the girls played sports.

	Sports	No Sports	TOTAL
Boys			
Girls			
TOTAL			

1. Complete the two-way table.

2. What is the relative frequency of a student playing sports? _____

3. What is the relative frequency of a boy playing sports? _____

4. Is there an association between being a boy and playing sports at Karen's school? Explain.

_____

_____

_____

_____

Aiden collected data from 80 students about whether they have siblings and whether they have pets.

	Siblings	No Siblings	TOTAL
Pets	49	21	70
No Pets	7	3	10
TOTAL	56	24	80

5. What is the relative frequency of a student having pets? _____

6. What is the relative frequency of a student with siblings having pets? _____

7. Is there an association between having siblings and having pets? Explain.

_____

_____

_____

_____

Problem Solving Connections

Give me a T! Annika asks several of her classmates to make a T with their bodies by standing up straight and putting their arms straight out to their sides. She measures their arm spans and their heights in inches. What associations can be made from the data she collects?

COMMON CORE

CC.8.SP.1
CC.8.SP.2
CC.8.SP.3
CC.8.SP.4

1 Making Scatter Plots

A Annika records her measurements in the table.

Boys		
Name	**Height (in.)**	**Arm Span (in.)**
George	60	$60\frac{1}{2}$
Hank	$52\frac{1}{4}$	50
Peter	60	59
Christopher	65	65
Girls		
Name	**Height (in.)**	**Arm Span (in.)**
Julie	$63\frac{1}{2}$	62
Louisa	55	55
Jan	62	$62\frac{1}{4}$
Kelly	50	$61\frac{3}{4}$

B Make a scatter plot using the data.

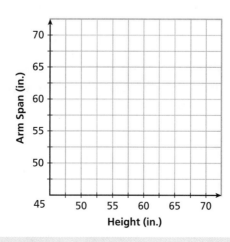

C What overall trends do you see in the scatter plot?

_____

_____

_____

D Do you see any outliers? Why might there be an outlier?

_____

_____

_____

2 Finding a Trend line

A Sketch a trend line on the scatter plot. (Hint: Because you will need to write an equation for the line later, it is a good idea to draw your line through data points, if possible.)

B How well does your trend line fit the data?

_____

_____

C Measure your height in inches. Use the trend line to predict your arm span.

_____

_____

D Identify two data points that your trend line goes through.

_____

_____

_____

E Calculate the slope of your trend line.

F Write an equation for the trend line in slope-intercept form.

G Use your trend line to interpolate how wide someone's arm span is if the individual is 58 inches tall.

H Choose a height for which you would have to extrapolate, and use your trend line to predict what the arm span would be.

I Under what circumstances might this trend line not be a good predictor of arm span?

_____

_____

_____

_____

3 Making a Two-Way Table

A Complete the two-way table using Annika's data.

	Arm Span Equal to Height	Arm Span Not Equal to Height	TOTAL
Boys			
Girls			
TOTAL			

B How can you check that you completed the table correctly?

_____

_____

_____

C What is the relative frequency of boys?

D What is the relative frequency of equal height and arm span for all students?

E What is the relative frequency of equal height and arm span among boys?

4 Answer the Question

A Does there appear to be an association between being a boy and having equal height and arm span? Explain.

_____

_____

_____

_____

B Why might this data set be misleading?

_____

_____

_____

C What conclusions can Annika draw from her data?

_____

_____

_____

Name _____ Class _____ Date _____

MULTIPLE CHOICE

1. Which graph shows a negative association?

A.

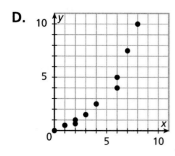

B.

C.

D.

2. For which type of association will a trend line **not** be very accurate?

F. linear association

G. nonlinear association

H. positive linear association

J. negative linear association

Rebecca played several games of cards with her brother. She made a scatter plot showing how many minutes each game lasted and how many points she scored during that game. Use the scatter plot for 3–5.

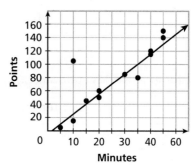

3. Using the trend line, how many points can Rebecca expect to score if the game lasts 25 minutes?

A. 25

B. 45

C. 70

D. 100

4. What is the equation for the trend line?

F. $y = 2x$

G. $y = 3x$

H. $y = 3x - 5$

J. $y = 3x + 5$

5. Using the equation for the trend line, how many points might Rebecca score in a game that lasts 100 minutes?

A. 95

B. 200

C. 205

D. 295

A survey of 50 adults asked whether the person had children and whether they had a cat. Use the table for 6–7.

	Cat	No cat	TOTAL
Children	5	27	
No children	16	2	
TOTAL	21	29	50

6. Of those surveyed, 64% said they do have children. Which values complete the last column of the table?

    F. Children: 64; No children: 36

    G. Children: 32; No children: 18

    H. Children: 25; No children: 25

    J. Children: 30; No children: 20

7. Which conclusion can be drawn?

    A. There appears to be an association between having no children and having a cat.

    B. The total number of people with cats is 32.

    C. There is no association between having children and having a cat.

    D. The relative frequency of people with no children is 18%.

FREE RESPONSE

Noah researched the weekly high temperature in his city. He chose several weeks between July and December to put in a table. (The first week of July was numbered Week 1 in Noah's source material.) Use this data for Questions 8–11.

Week	High Temp (°F)	Week	High Temp (°F)
16	78	12	78
25	55	7	95
3	100	10	84
17	65	9	90
13	75	15	74
5	90	21	62

8. Use Noah's data to make a scatter plot.

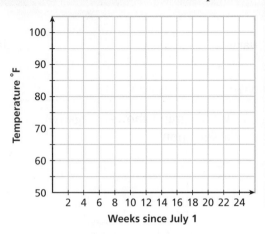

9. What type of association is shown on the scatterplot? Explain.

_____

_____

_____

_____

_____

10. Draw a trend line on the scatter plot.

11. Remember that Week 1 represents the first week of July so Week 25 represents a week in December. Would your trend line lend to good predictions of high temperatures in May of the next year? Explain.

_____

_____

_____

_____

_____

_____

Correlation of *On Core Mathematics Grade 8* to the Common Core State Standards

The Number System	Citations
CC.8.NS.1 Understand informally that every number has a decimal expansion; the rational numbers are those with decimal expansions that terminate in 0s or eventually repeat. Know that other numbers are called irrational.	pp. 19–22
CC.8.NS.2 Use rational approximations of irrational numbers to compare the size of irrational numbers, locate them approximately on a number line diagram, and estimate the value of expressions (e.g., π^2).	pp. 23–26

Expressions and Equations	Citations
CC.8.EE.1 Know and apply the properties of integer exponents to generate equivalent numerical expressions.	pp. 3–6, 27–30
CC.8.EE.2 Use square root and cube root symbols to represent solutions to equations of the form $x^2 = p$ and $x^3 = p$, where p is a positive rational number. Evaluate square roots of small perfect squares and cube roots of small perfect cubes. Know that $\sqrt{2}$ is irrational.	pp. 15–18, 23–26
CC.8.EE.3 Use numbers expressed in the form of a single digit times an integer power of 10 to estimate very large or very small quantities, and to express how many times as much one is than the other.	pp. 7–10, 27–30
CC.8.EE.4 Perform operations with numbers expressed in scientific notation, including problems where both decimal and scientific notation are used. Use scientific notation and choose units of appropriate size for measurements of very large or very small quantities (e.g., use millimeters per year for seafloor spreading). Interpret scientific notation that has been generated by technology.	pp. 11–14, 27–30
CC.8.EE.5 Graph proportional relationships, interpreting the unit rate as the slope of the graph. Compare two different proportional relationships represented in different ways.	pp. 39–42, 43–46, 53–56, 61–64
CC.8.EE.6 Use similar triangles to explain why the slope m is the same between any two distinct points on a non-vertical line in the coordinate plane; derive the equation $y = mx$ for a line through the origin and the equation $y = mx + b$ for a line intercepting the vertical axis at b.	pp. 47–48, 61–64, 137–140
CC.8.EE.7 Solve linear equations in one variable. a. Give examples of linear equations in one variable with one solution, infinitely many solutions, or no solutions. Show which of these possibilities is the case by successively transforming the given equation into simpler forms, until an equivalent equation of the form $x = a$, $a = a$, or $a = b$ results (where a and b are different numbers). b. Solve linear equations with rational number coefficients, including equations whose solutions require expanding expressions using the distributive property and collecting like terms.	pp. 69–72, 73–74, 83–86

CC.8.EE.8 Analyze and solve pairs of simultaneous linear equations. a. Understand that solutions to a system of two linear equations in two variables correspond to points of intersection of their graphs, because points of intersection satisfy both equations simultaneously. b. Solve systems of two linear equations in two variables algebraically, and estimate solutions by graphing the equations. Solve simple cases by inspection. c. Solve real-world and mathematical problems leading to two linear equations in two variables.	pp. 75–78, 79–82, 83–86

Functions	**Citations**
CC.8.F.1 Understand that a function is a rule that assigns to each input exactly one output. The graph of a function is the set of ordered pairs consisting of an input and the corresponding output.	pp. 35–38, 61–64
CC.8.F.2 Compare properties of two functions each represented in a different way (algebraically, graphically, numerically in tables, or by verbal descriptions).	pp. 53–56
CC.8.F.3 Interpret the equation $y = mx + b$ as defining a linear function, whose graph is a straight line; give examples of functions that are not linear.	pp. 39–42, 47–48, 49–52, 61–64
CC.8.F.4 Construct a function to model a linear relationship between two quantities. Determine the rate of change and initial value of the function from a description of a relationship or from two (x, y) values, including reading these from a table or from a graph. Interpret the rate of change and initial value of a linear function in terms of the situation it models, and in terms of its graph or a table of values.	pp. 49–52, 53–56, 61–64
CC.8.F.5 Describe qualitatively the functional relationship between two quantities by analyzing a graph (e.g., where the function is increasing or decreasing, linear or nonlinear). Sketch a graph that exhibits the qualitative features of a function that has been described verbally.	pp. 57–60, 61–64

Geometry	**Citations**
CC.8.G.1 Verify experimentally the properties of rotations, reflections, and translations: a. Lines are taken to lines, and line segments to line segments of the same length. b. Angles are taken to angles of the same measure. c. Parallel lines are taken to parallel lines.	pp. 95–96, 105–108
CC.8.G.2 Understand that a two-dimensional figure is congruent to another if the second can be obtained from the first by a sequence of rotations, reflections, and translations; given two congruent figures, describe a sequence that exhibits the congruence between them.	pp. 97–98, 105–108
CC.8.G.3 Describe the effect of dilations, translations, rotations, and reflections on two-dimensional figures using coordinates.	pp. 91–94, 99–102, 105–108
CC.8.G.4 Understand that a two-dimensional figure is similar to another if the second can be obtained from the first by a sequence of rotations, reflections, translations, and dilations; given two similar two-dimensional figures, describe a sequence that exhibits the similarity between them.	pp. 103–104, 105–108
CC.8.G.5 Use informal arguments to establish facts about the angle sum and exterior angle of triangles, about the angles created when parallel lines are cut by a transversal, and the angle-angle criterion for similarity of triangles.	pp. 113–116, 117–120, 121–124, 137–140
CC.8.G.6 Explain a proof of the Pythagorean Theorem and its converse.	pp. 125–126, 131–132, 137–140

CC.8.G.7 Apply the Pythagorean Theorem to determine unknown side lengths in right triangles in real-world and mathematical problems in two and three dimensions.	pp. 127–130, 137–140
CC.8.G.8 Apply the Pythagorean Theorem to find the distance between two points in a coordinate system.	pp. 127–130, 137–140
CC.8.G.9 Know the formulas for the volumes of cones, cylinders, and spheres and use them to solve real-world and mathematical problems.	pp. 133–136, 137–140
Statistics and Probability	**Citations**
CC.8.SP.1 Construct and interpret scatter plots for bivariate measurement data to investigate patterns of association between two quantities. Describe patterns such as clustering, outliers, positive or negative association, linear association, and nonlinear association.	pp. 145–148, 157–160
CC.8.SP.2 Know that straight lines are widely used to model relationships between two quantitative variables. For scatter plots that suggest a linear association, informally fit a straight line, and informally assess the model fit by judging the closeness of the data points to the line.	pp. 149–152, 157–160
CC.8.SP.3 Use the equation of a linear model to solve problems in the context of bivariate measurement data, interpreting the slope and intercept.	pp. 149–152, 157–160
CC.8.SP.4 Understand that patterns of association can also be seen in bivariate categorical data by displaying frequencies and relative frequencies in a two-way table. Construct and interpret a two-way table summarizing data on two categorical variables collected from the same subjects. Use relative frequencies calculated for rows or columns to describe possible association between the two variables.	pp. 153–156, 157–160